SPREAD TOO THIN

ellen miller

SPREAD *too* THIN

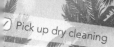

OPTING *out of* FRANTIC LIVING

OPTING *in to* LASTING *peace*

TYNDALE
MOMENTUM®

The nonfiction imprint of
Tyndale House Publishers, Inc.

Visit Tyndale online at www.tyndale.com.

Visit Tyndale Momentum online at www.tyndalemomentum.com.

TYNDALE, Tyndale Momentum, and Tyndale's quill logo are registered trademarks of Tyndale House Publishers, Inc. The Tyndale Momentum logo is a trademark of Tyndale House Publishers, Inc. Tyndale Momentum is the nonfiction imprint of Tyndale House Publishers, Inc., Carol Stream, Illinois.

Spread Too Thin: Opting Out of Frantic Living. Opting In to Lasting Peace.

Copyright © 2018 by Ellen Miller. All rights reserved.

Cover illustrations are the property of their respective copyright holders, and all rights are reserved. Pencils copyright © DoozyDo/Shutterstock; notebook copyright © Olesya Kuznetsova/Shutterstock; smartphone copyright © Lemberg Vector studio/Shutterstock; glasses copyright © M. Stasy/Shutterstock; calendar copyright © Orgus88/Shutterstock; calendar copyright © Orgus88/Shutterstock; coffee mug copyright © vladwel/Adobe Stock; palm trees copyright © maryvoo/Adobe Stock; folder copyright © msgrigorievna/Adobe Stock; coffee cup stains © KsushaArt/Shutterstock.

Author photograph by Jin Kim Studio, copyright © 2016. All rights reserved.

Designed by Julie Chen

Unless otherwise indicated, all Scripture quotations are taken from the *Holy Bible*, New Living Translation, copyright © 1996, 2004, 2015 by Tyndale House Foundation. Used by permission of Tyndale House Publishers, Inc., Carol Stream, Illinois 60188. All rights reserved.

Scripture quotations marked ESV are taken from *The Holy Bible*, English Standard Version® (ESV®), copyright © 2001 by Crossway, a publishing ministry of Good News Publishers. Used by permission. All rights reserved.

Scripture quotations marked KJV are taken from the *Holy Bible*, King James Version.

Scripture quotations marked MSG are taken from *THE MESSAGE*, copyright © 1993, 1994, 1995, 1996, 2000, 2001, 2002 by Eugene H. Peterson. Used by permission of NavPress. All rights reserved. Represented by Tyndale House Publishers, Inc.

Scripture quotations marked NASB are taken from the New American Standard Bible,® copyright © 1960, 1962, 1963, 1968, 1971, 1972, 1973, 1975, 1977, 1995 by The Lockman Foundation. Used by permission.

Scripture quotations marked NIV are taken from the Holy Bible, *New International Version*,® *NIV*.® Copyright © 1973, 1978, 1984, 2011 by Biblica, Inc.® Used by permission. All rights reserved worldwide.

Scripture quotations marked NRSV are taken from the New Revised Standard Version Bible, copyright © 1989, Division of Christian Education of the National Council of the Churches of Christ in the United States of America. Used by permission. All rights reserved.

Scripture quotations marked TLB are taken from *The Living Bible*, copyright © 1971 by Tyndale House Foundation. Used by permission of Tyndale House Publishers, Inc., Carol Stream, Illinois 60188. All rights reserved.

For information about special discounts for bulk purchases, please contact Tyndale House Publishers at csresponse@tyndale.com, or call 1-800-323-9400.

ISBN 978-1-4964-1941-5

Printed in the United States of America

24   23   22   21   20   19   18
7   6   5   4   3   2

FOR STEVE.

MY INSPIRATION. MY ENCOURAGER. MY LOVE.

INTRODUCTION

THE LATE PASTOR ADRIAN ROGERS once said, "If Satan can't make you bad, he'll make you busy." *Oh my.* If this is true, he's got his hooks set in a whole society of American women, including me!

At every stage of life and within every demographic—single ladies to those who are married, working gals to stay-at-home moms, freshly minted college graduates to retirees—I hear the same resounding chant: "I'm overwhelmed. I'm exhausted. I'm spread too thin." From daybreak to sunset, many of us obsessively and frantically cross items off a to-do list that is as long as our leg—only to fall into bed at the end of the day feeling unproductive, unfulfilled, and sometimes even inconsequential in the grand scheme of life. These "distractions"—the things that must be done and even those things we want to do—often prevent us from living a deeply rewarding life. If not managed carefully, even the activities and hobbies we enjoy can override our happiness and rob us of a sense of extraordinary peace.

In the Gospel of John, Jesus said, "I came that they may have life and have it *abundantly*."[1] Jesus did not lay down his life so that we might spend our waking moments stressed out and diluted. He died for our sins so that we might have eternal life and so that we might live a rich, meaningful, glorious life while we're here. What disrespect we show when we allow *busy* to trump our *blessed*.

I feel that you and I were destined for this divine appointment by the fact that you are sitting with this book in your hands—a book that God has had on my heart to write for several years. Written specifically for women who care deeply, love unconditionally, extend themselves selflessly, and work tirelessly, I look forward to our honest exchange about those things beyond our choices or obligations that have us wrung out—such as the baggage that often contributes to and controls the disposition of our hearts, our state of mind, our physical well-being, and most importantly, the condition of our souls. When we sacrifice caring for and feeding any or all of these areas, our patience with others declines, the quality of our love withers, and the extent of our faith becomes shallow. When we're spread too thin, we have a tendency to go flat for everyone, especially ourselves.

As we explore together what drives us, both positively and negatively, we'll likely find some commonality. In the sections "Heart Conditioning" and "Mind Games You Can Win," we will tackle emotions, sins, virtues, and errant thinking that can lead us to exhaustion. Some topics in this section may stir something deep within you— a conviction, perhaps, that an attitude needs to change, or a desire, maybe, to recommit your life to those long-held truths and values that somehow got entombed in the busyness of your life. Negative emotions or thoughts that have held you hostage might be illuminated, allowing you to free yourself from their clutches. And when you feel the stir of the Holy Spirit, I hope you won't suppress it, but instead allow him to move you as you evaluate what attitudes and habits you have that might need to change. If you feel like you're at the end of your rope, I hope you will find the confidence and insight to let go.

But of course, letting go of the rope can be scary if you think there's no one there to catch you! In the sections "Strength Training for the Long Run" and "Soul-Searching for the Abundant Life," we'll look into how exhaustion hijacks some of the most gratifying moments of our days and how we can reclaim our joy by following a better way. Actually, it's the only way. When we let go of our rope and *choose* to live an abundant life with Christ—we find the fall is exhilarating; his net is proven.

As you journey with me, I invite you to celebrate your wins in Christ. Take no pride in your own victory, but praise God for the blessings of discernment, conviction, redemption, and discipline. Honor and revere these gifts and look for more ways to optimize them in order to live an uncommon life of joy—regardless of your circumstances. We know we are living well when our thoughts and actions glorify God, transforming us from a state of operating within our own power to operating within his.

My process for writing this book began each morning in prayer, humbly asking God to reveal only his desires for your heart, not my own. My petition was for the ability to declare to you, in the clearest way possible, the love, the power, and the promise that is yours through Christ—for I have not the words, but I know he does. Written within these pages are those he has pressed on my mind and heart to share. Now the work is between you and the Holy Spirit. Thus I leave you with this Scripture, the prayer I have prayed over you for months. It is a prayer of enlightenment and empowerment, that you might be encouraged to let go of those things that have you spread too thin in order to live an extraordinary life with all that is at your disposal through him.

I PRAY THAT FROM HIS GLORIOUS, UNLIMITED RESOURCES HE WILL EMPOWER YOU WITH INNER STRENGTH THROUGH HIS SPIRIT. THEN CHRIST WILL MAKE HIS HOME IN YOUR HEARTS AS YOU TRUST IN HIM. YOUR ROOTS WILL GROW DOWN INTO GOD'S LOVE AND KEEP YOU STRONG. AND MAY YOU HAVE THE POWER TO UNDERSTAND, AS ALL GOD'S PEOPLE SHOULD, HOW WIDE, HOW LONG, HOW HIGH, AND HOW DEEP HIS LOVE IS. MAY YOU EXPERIENCE THE LOVE OF CHRIST, THOUGH IT IS TOO GREAT TO UNDERSTAND FULLY. THEN YOU WILL BE MADE COMPLETE WITH ALL THE FULLNESS OF LIFE AND POWER THAT COMES FROM GOD. NOW ALL GLORY TO GOD, WHO IS ABLE, THROUGH HIS MIGHTY POWER AT WORK WITHIN US, TO ACCOMPLISH INFINITELY MORE THAN WE MIGHT ASK OR THINK.

EPHESIANS 3:16-20

In absolute awe of his incredible greatness,

Ellen

PART 1

HEART
Conditioning

DAY 1

OVERWHELMED

Beware the barrenness of a busy life.
SOCRATES

I AM OVERWHELMED. As I write to you today from my home office, I have a half dozen men working downstairs, repairing drywall in our home that is only a year old. As the crew labors to perfect our walls, another crew is outside, making repairs to our irrigation system. This entails digging up our yard, purchasing new plants, and starting all over again. Did I mention this house is only a year old?

As I write to you today while overseeing contractors, I am making final edits to my book *Lord, Have Mercy: Help and Hope for Moms on Their Last Nerve*, which by the time you're reading this will have launched in April of 2017. I have never experienced writing a book while putting the finishing touches on another. I am thankful that the time management of this endeavor is coming together, but I'm finding the allocation of brain cells to be a challenge.

As I write to you today while overseeing contractors and editing a book, I'm also working on our company's three-year strategic plan. To do this, I must lead our executives through a well-structured process that requires me to work weeks ahead of them in order to keep the timeline on track. It's fun, but it's also difficult as I stretch myself and my team professionally.

As I write to you today while overseeing contractors, editing a book, and working on our company's three-year plan, I am also coleading a women's Bible study. This dedicated time of researching and reflecting on God's Word is like warm sourdough bread (with lots of butter!) for my hungry soul. However, I'm pretty sure it is also contributing to my sleep deprivation.

As I write to you today while overseeing contractors, editing a book, working on our company's three-year plan, and preparing for the next Bible study class, I am helping my husband, Steve, care for his mom, who will be released from the hospital today. In addition, I am preparing myself mentally and physically for our granddaughter's monthly sleepover. (One does not await eight-year-old Ava's arrival; this child is a ball of energy, so one must be *ready*!) The emotional, mental, and physical demands of supporting and loving my family play a pivotal role in my "overwhelmedness" (I know this is not a word, but it should be) on any given day. Nothing can zap me like their disappointment. Nothing can wilt me like an exchange that is anything but joyful and God-honoring.

I am overwhelmed today by the many commitments I have made and the many needs of our family. Some are very good—fulfilling, stimulating, and glorifying to God. However, some have led to my emotional, mental, and physical exhaustion. And all would leave me completely depleted and spread too thin if I wasn't overwhelmed by something far greater than the busyness of life—the grace of God. Every day I'm humbled by his forgiveness, grateful for his counsel through his holy Word, and captivated by his love for me. Because of him I embrace the "overwhelmedness" of not just a busy, but an abundant life.

As we begin our ninety-day journey together, I have a question for you:

o Are you overwhelmed by living in a state of exhaustion, or are you overwhelmed by the grace and glory of God?

O GOD, LISTEN TO MY CRY! HEAR MY PRAYER! FROM THE ENDS OF THE EARTH, I CRY TO YOU FOR HELP WHEN MY HEART IS OVERWHELMED. LEAD ME TO THE TOWERING ROCK OF SAFETY, FOR YOU ARE MY SAFE REFUGE.

PSALM 61:1-3

One state leads to a life of scarcity—days that are a busy, unfulfilling blur. The other state provides a profoundly rewarding life, despite the distractions—even when a landscaping crew is digging up your autumn sage while in full bloom.

DAY 2

WE NEED A FIRE

To live is the rarest thing in the world. Most people exist, that is all.
OSCAR WILDE

STEPPING INTO OUR rented casita in Santa Fe, Steve and I put down our bags and began touring the place. We had chosen this particular home for our mini retreat because it was cute and comfy, located in town, and walking distance to galleries and restaurants. But what had really caught my eye when I researched this property weeks prior was the large wood-burning fireplace.

To take the October chill out of the air, Steve made haste in building a cozy fire for us. Rummaging through the kindling stacked outside the back door, he carefully picked through the sticks and twigs to find those dry enough to easily catch fire. After arranging them in the fireplace, he struck a match, threw it in, and waited patiently. As the fire took hold, he placed dry logs on top, and a crackling blaze ensued. Dragging a comfy, overstuffed chair and ottoman closer to the fireplace, he helped me "set up my office." With my notebook computer perched on my lap and a cup of tea only an arm's reach away, I was good to go for an afternoon of writing while he went into town to scout out dinner.

The dancing flames, glowing embers, and I worked beautifully together throughout the afternoon, but only because we were prepared. We had both been kindled.

Living the uncommon life God has called us to is like building a fire. We have to be well prepped in order to get our flame going. Wet or green wood will not light, and logs that are not well seasoned will not perform to their highest function. And neither will we if our hearts have not been kindled by his Word.

I believe that deep within us our hearts yearn for a gratifying life rather than a diluted existence of never-ending activity. Our minds and bodies long to be still and quiet instead of spinning in the constant state of motion that we allow. Our souls hunger for a revival, for the abundant life God has promised, rather than the daily drudgery of what we have accepted as normal and routine. But to live an abundant life, we must condition our hearts. We must light a fire of desire for something new, something better. And with that desire must come the careful gathering of the kindling of Scripture, the patient building of the flame of understanding, and the quietness of spirit to enjoy the glow of his glory.

THE THIEF COMES ONLY TO STEAL AND KILL AND DESTROY;
I CAME THAT THEY MAY HAVE LIFE, AND HAVE IT ABUNDANTLY.
JOHN 10:10, NASB

Christ gave his very life, dying an excruciating death, so that you and I may have the opportunity and promise of an abundant life. The Father and Son paid a huge ransom for this great inheritance that awaits us here on earth and for eternity, yet we continue to live sparsely as paupers rather than richly as queens.

As you consider this gift of abundant life given to us through Jesus, take a moment to answer these questions:

o Have you thought about this rich inheritance that has been promised to you?
o Have you claimed it?
o If not, what lifestyle changes might be required for you to cash in?

It might be time to gather some twigs and light a match. When the truth burns within us, the abundant life begins.

DAY 3

RESTORATION

*My deepest awareness of myself is that I am deeply loved by Jesus Christ
and I have done nothing to earn it or deserve it.*
BRENNAN MANNING, *The Ragamuffin Gospel*

STEVE AND I ARE serial remodelers and builders. We love having the
opportunity and challenge of breathing new life into old homes. One
of our many houses over the years was a midcentury modern home
built in 1960. This house was a complete throwback to another era;
you could hear Frank Sinatra singing from the minute you hit the
front door (and the stereo wasn't even on)! With walls of stone and
glass, and multiple levels to deal with, this house was a wreck when
we bought her. Oh, her bones were good. The floor plan and vaulted
ceilings, along with the room sizes and proportion, were perfect. The
old girl even sat on a gorgeous wooded lot. But her white stone walls
had yellowed from thirty-five years of cigarette smoke, her single-pane
glass made her drafty, and the kitchen was something out of, well . . .
1960! She needed some serious restoration.

But then sometimes we do, too, don't we? We have good "bones"—
we're good people at our core—but sometimes those bones get creaky,
stiff, and even stressed to the point of breaking. Answering the demands
of our family and friends can take its toll on us emotionally. We hear
ourselves snap at someone we love dearly, be dismissive, or even give
a sarcastic reply, and we think, *Who said that?* or *What's come over
me?* When the edginess becomes a habit, we might think, *I don't even
like the person I have become.* I know this because it has happened to
me—more than once. Then I begin to feel guilty. And then I mentally

berate myself. And then I feel like a loser. And then, well . . . you get the picture.

It is in these moments when we're spread too thin by our own commitments and the demands of others that we must remember two things: First, we are sinners—we're gonna mess up, and likely we're going to feel bad when we do. And second, we're loved by Christ regardless of what we have or have not done. Even though we're getting older by the moment, just like our old girl in East Dallas, Christ has everything he needs to restore us to the beauty we were created for, if we'll open up the doors of our hearts and let him scrub us clean. The restoration of our emotional health begins when we stop to recognize those things that contribute to our emotional frailty. Our joy is revived in the simple things when we stop to acknowledge them and become grateful for them in the moment. Our passion for living is renewed when we decide to hush that constant hum of doing, thinking, and worrying, and instead listen to God's faithful promises.

As you consider your personal revitalization project, take a few moments to answer these questions:

- Do you see how being spread too thin affects your emotional stability?
- Have you ever thought, *I don't like who I've become?*
- What areas of your heart would you like to see restored or given new life?

RESTORE TO ME THE JOY OF YOUR SALVATION AND GRANT ME A WILLING SPIRIT, TO SUSTAIN ME.
PSALM 51:12, NIV

It took a long time, a lot of Scrubbing Bubbles, and an army of contractors, but we brought that classic home in East Dallas back to her original glory. Your restoration in Christ will bring you back to yours, too.

DAY 4

UNINTENDED CONSEQUENCES

A consciousness of wrongdoing is the first step to salvation . . .
you have to catch yourself doing it before you can correct it.
SENECA THE YOUNGER

IT WAS LIKELY A BIT cool on that beautiful July evening in 2016 in Garrapata State Park, California. I can only imagine the crackling fire offered a cozy setting for the hikers who gathered around it. They had positioned themselves at a scenic spot, where Soberanes Creek meets another nearby waterway. To this day, it isn't clear if the two-by-two-foot campfire was built by one person or more; however, whoever was responsible must have watched with horror at the unintended consequences of their actions: Hundreds evacuated; two thousand homes in the path of the wildfire, with fifty-seven homes completely destroyed; more than one hundred thousand acres scorched; and one life lost in what would soon be known as the Soberanes fire.

The campfire was illegal. This the hikers had to know due to the serious and well-publicized drought conditions in California. But they ignored the warning signs. They wanted what they wanted—what they thought seemed reasonable—a lovely fire on a chilly evening.

It's easy to sit in judgment of the guilty party, but I'm afraid we often operate from a similar mind-set. We desire, strive for, and sometimes even convince ourselves that we deserve more, while ignoring the warning signs that our actions are scorching the abundant life intended for us. When we become overly focused on accomplishing our personal, familial, and professional goals, we can unconsciously adopt negative attitudes, wayward thinking, and bad habits that rob us of peace and joy. The foundational motive of the goal—the original spark of happiness—gets unwittingly displaced by selfishness that leads to damaged relationships. Or it is replaced with day-to-day busyness that leads to exhaustion. It's like the campfire—we intend the outcome of our goals for good, but getting there can lead to an aftermath of personal and spiritual destruction.

This heart condition often leads to barren living. It produces an anxiousness that we allow to slowly creep into our psyches and that later becomes our basic mode of operation. This anxiousness is the tinder for a fire that will not light us up, but will, over time, burn us out. However, searching our hearts objectively opens a path for the Holy Spirit to come in and help us identify and extinguish this flame of destruction in order to claim and live the fulfilling life Christ has promised—a life filled with mornings in which we awaken with contented hearts that have finally tamed unbridled cravings; a life in which anxious, restless nights are replaced by the sweet spirit of peace that only comes from walking in faith. Does this sound like a heavenly dream? It's actually yours, if you want it.

Here are some "heart check" questions for you today:

o Are there warning signs in your life, such as rocky relationships or a health condition, that you have been ignoring?
o Can you identify wayward thinking or bad habits that consistently rob you of joy and peace?
o Is an anxious spirit affecting your daily interactions and thoughts?
o Have you called on the Holy Spirit to help you with this condition of your heart?

SEARCH ME, O GOD, AND KNOW MY HEART; TEST ME AND KNOW MY ANXIOUS THOUGHTS.

PSALM 139:23

If the hikers responsible for the Soberanes fire are ever identified, they will likely face charges of negligence and possibly manslaughter for the devastation they wreaked. Let's not ignore our own warning signs. Unintended consequences can rob us of the abundant life.

DAY 5

HUNGRY FOR MORE

I recently learned a new word: insatiable. That's me.

NATALIA MAKAROVA

MANY OF US WOULD probably not describe ourselves as having a ravenous need or a persistent yearning for more (although I did just buy a new pair of Nike tennis shoes that are so comfortable and cute, I have convinced myself that I *need* a second pair).

But, as Americans, many of us lean to the side of materialism and ladder-climbing—investing more money and time than we should in the pursuit of acquiring external things and professional advancement. This is a common issue we must work daily to counter to prevent our desires from becoming an insatiable appetite for more. It's this mind-set and behavior that is a threat to experiencing the life Christ has promised.

Many years ago I met a child who had been diagnosed with Prader-Willi syndrome. One of the debilitating symptoms of this genetic disorder is an endless feeling of hunger. My heart broke for the little boy who had just finished his meal but sat weeping because he was still so hungry. His parents had fed him, but the little guy's mind could not register that his tummy had been filled.

How often do we approach life in a similar manner? We enjoy our current jobs, but we have an endless hunger for a promotion. Our boss has just given us a wonderful review, but we're already pining for the next bit of recognition. This endless striving feeds our frantic life. So often we're deceived because a rewarding, satisfying life is disguised as a buffet of "more."

But unlike my little friend, our condition is not associated with a malfunction in the hypothalamus; ours is a malfunction of the heart. Our Father has fed us everything we could possibly need and more, but we often feel or act as though we're starving. Our insatiable appetites drive us to the end of a rope, where we lose sight of the things we do have that are good and meaningful and eternal. And where there is an absence of gratitude for our blessings (including but beyond material things), there is no lasting peace. To claim our eternal inheritance, we have to let go of the worldly things we've grasped so tightly and cling to his unending devotion, perfect peace, and promises given to us by trusting that he knows better than we do about those things that are truly good and perfect for our lives. Sister, sometimes that corner office or relationship with that particular guy is not what's best for us. Trust God—he knows the disastrous outcomes we cannot see and has blessings in store for us that we cannot even imagine.

Let's do a quick gut check on our insatiable appetites:

○ Do you find yourself thinking obsessively about how you can get ahead?
○ Do you think a prestigious job, a different social circle, or a nicer neighborhood will "fill" you?
○ Are you convinced that something, some person, or some achievement will bring you the joy you lack?

THE WORLD OFFERS ONLY A CRAVING FOR PHYSICAL PLEASURE, A CRAVING FOR EVERYTHING WE SEE, AND PRIDE IN OUR ACHIEVEMENTS AND POSSESSIONS. THESE ARE NOT FROM THE FATHER, BUT ARE FROM THIS WORLD.

1 JOHN 2:16

This heart condition that causes us to be spread too thin has also been called lust and gluttony. Feed your appetite and cravings with eternal nutrients, not empty temporal snacks.

DAY 6

THE BOY WITH THE BACKPACK

I have so much to do that I shall spend the first three hours in prayer.
MARTIN LUTHER

LAST SUMMER, Steve and I vacationed in San Miguel de Allende, Mexico. A UNESCO World Heritage destination, the area is rich in history, architecture, and art, as was evidenced by the Parroquia de San Miguel Arcángel, the local church. Built in the early 1700s and given an updated facade in the late 1800s, it serves as a majestic centerpiece for the quaint city. La Parroquia—the parish church—as it's most commonly called, is stunning. The exterior, clad in pink limestone, changes colors throughout the day as the sun rises and sets. But as we toured the church, there was nothing more breathtaking than the boy with the backpack.

Steve and I had woven our way through the church, taking in the culturally significant art and architectural detail, and headed for the main church doors that serve as both the entrance to and exit from the sanctuary. There, kneeling at the second pew, was a young man no older than seventeen or eighteen. His head was bowed, his lips moved in fervent prayer, and tears were streaming down his face. As I silently walked past, praying with him and for him, tears flooded my eyes. His need to drop to his knees was so imperative, he hadn't even taken the time to remove his overstuffed backpack that burdened his shoulders. Watching him, I thought at that moment, *This is the way we should pray. Urgently. Passionately. Reverently.*

But so often we're *too busy.* Too busy to take a few quiet moments, too busy to kneel, and certainly too busy to pour out our hearts.

Instead, we say a prayer as we run out the door because that's all our diluted lives allow. But how desperately we need to stop and pray like that young man.

I appreciate the fact that many of my readers are not "church ladies," so the concept of fervent prayer might be a bit confusing. Let me share with you a well-known method called ACTS, a favorite of mine, that many Christians practice. The four-step guide goes like this:

A: *Adoration.* Open your prayer with how much you love God and respect him. Praise him for who he is. Acknowledge that he is God. Note: You might begin to feel very small.

C: *Confession.* Open your heart to God and tell him you're sorry for something you said or thought or did that you know was not pleasing to him. By asking for his forgiveness, you'll know you don't need to carry your sins anymore.

T: *Thanksgiving.* State clearly your gratitude to God for loving you, protecting you, providing for your salvation from hell, and for all his provisions. Just say thanks. You might begin to tear up, and if so, that's okay.

S: *Supplication.* Ask for his mercy, grace, and blessings on your work, family, and friends. Ask specifically about the challenges and areas where you need his divine intervention. When you feel empowered and relieved, you'll know he's already at work.

Here are a couple of questions for you to ponder today:

○ If prayer is key to achieving this new standard of living, are you willing to prioritize your prayer time?

○ When you pray, will you attempt to use the ACTS method, which begins with a time of pure worship and thanksgiving, rather than a list of requests?

Hear me as I pray, O Lord. Be merciful and answer me!
My heart has heard you say, "Come and talk with me."
And my heart responds, "Lord, I am coming."

PSALM 27:7-8

I can't help wondering what the boy with the backpack was praying. Were those tears of praise for an answered prayer? Was he petitioning God on behalf of someone else? Was he asking forgiveness or maybe saying a prayer of repentance and rededication? I will never know. Oh, but I do know he was in the company of the Almighty.

DAY 7

IT'S THE GREENS

Worry is not believing God will get it right,
and bitterness is believing God got it wrong.

TIM KELLER

LAST WEEK I PULLED from the refrigerator and assembled everything I needed for a scrumptious salad: deep-red cherry tomatoes still hanging from a vine, a crisp English cucumber, a sweet purple onion, a thinly sliced bell pepper (orange as a pumpkin in October), and my favorite salad splurge—avocado. I tossed the "goody" ingredients with the "base"—a mixed concoction of romaine, radicchio, and arugula—and topped it all with a light vinaigrette. I don't want to brag, but the salad was gorgeous; it looked like spring in a bowl! Unfortunately it tasted like how my grandmother's quilt smells (a family heirloom that has been sitting in storage for more than forty years).

Although all of the vegetables were fresh, the lettuces were bitter. So bitter, in fact, that my delicious toppings would not disguise the harsh taste. Everything yummy and creative and beautiful in the salad was completely overwhelmed by the darn greens! Just a few bites in, I knew I couldn't stomach the rest. Sister, a bitter heart can overpower everything good around us, too, if we're not careful.

Dr. Stephen A. Diamond, a writer for *Psychology Today*, states, "*Bitterness*, which I define as a chronic and pervasive state of smoldering resentment, is one of the most destructive and toxic of human emotions."[2] A "pervasive state of smoldering resentment" sure sounds like a heart-stopper to me! And, toxic! This man, an expert in the field, calls bitterness a poison, and I believe him. I've watched many a beautiful woman turn ugly from the inside out. Bitterness starts with a crushing disappointment or a deep hurt that, over time, is allowed by its "host" to fester. The toxin simmers and stews in our hearts, coming to a slow boil that eventually cooks our joy. Make no mistake, this heart condition will kill any and all hope of living a life of lasting peace.

Resolving a disappointment or, worse, a dream lost, is required to embrace a life lived abundantly. I know of no one who operates in states of joy and bitterness simultaneously. It's like my salad of tasty toppings and harsh greens: The two don't mix. Bitterness will overpower everything meaningful to us until we decide we cannot keep living this way. It is then that we must petition Christ to heal our hearts so that we might recognize and claim the joy he gives us through our inheritance.

Could the poison of bitterness be hindering your broken heart from healing? Ask yourself,

o Who or what in my life causes me to be resentful?
o Is there anything beneficial to be gained by holding on to this?
o What would be the worst thing that could happen if I just laid this down at the feet of Christ?

EACH HEART KNOWS ITS OWN BITTERNESS, AND NO ONE ELSE CAN FULLY SHARE ITS JOY.
PROVERBS 14:10

The inheritance of abundance is ours to savor. Don't leave the good stuff on your plate.

DAY 8

PARDON ME?

There are only two ways to live your life. One is as though nothing is a miracle. The other is as though everything is a miracle.

ATTRIBUTED TO ALBERT EINSTEIN

IN THE SUMMER OF 1993 I was working for a technology retailer when Microsoft, our largest supplier of new products (and thus the driver of consumer traffic to our stores), shared with us that their new release of Microsoft Windows would be delayed. This huge problem was quickly handed to me to correct.

"Pardon me?" I asked my manager incredulously. "What can I do about this?" I couldn't write code to help Microsoft move up their release date by nine months! But, like it or not, the assignment was mine. For seventy-two hours, I panicked. What in the world was *I*, even in all my self-sufficiency, going to do? Looking back on this moment now, I see how my own story correlates with another found in Judges 6:11-23.[3] It goes like this:

One day, a man named Gideon was greeted by an angel, who said to him, "The LORD is with you, mighty warrior." Well, I don't know about you, but if I was Gideon, I'd be *giddy* to learn that God sent an angel to visit me and to know that God was on my side. But Gideon wasn't sold. He replied, "Pardon me, my lord, but if the LORD is with us, why has all this happened to us? Where are all his wonders that our ancestors told us about when they said, 'Did not the LORD bring us up out of Egypt?' But now the LORD has abandoned us and given us into the hand of Midian."

God, being *so* God, spoke patiently through the angel, saying (and I'm paraphrasing here), "I've given you what you need to save Israel. I've got your back!" But that wasn't good enough for Gideon. So he said, "Pardon me, my lord, but how can I save Israel? My clan is the weakest in Manasseh, and I am the least in my family."

Even though God just said he was with him, Gideon couldn't believe it. *Again*, the angel, speaking for the Lord, said, "I will be with you, and you will strike down all the Midianites, leaving none alive." Well, you'd think that would seal the deal, right? Oh no. Gideon replied, "If now I have found favor in your eyes, give me a sign that it is really you talking to me."

Lord, have mercy—Gideon is just like us. We all want a big, flashing sign that reads, "THIS IS THE WORD OF GOD! THIS IS WHAT YOU'RE SUPPOSED TO DO."

The story continues as Gideon prepares the angel an offering. The angel of the Lord touches the offering with his staff and fire flares from the rock, consuming the sacrifice. Of course, with this miracle, Gideon now believes. The angel then disappears, and God says, "Peace! Do not be afraid. You are not going to die." What God was saying to Gideon and what he's saying to us is "I've got your back. Of course you are not self-sufficient. I know you can't do this on your own. It's why I always show up."

Considering Gideon's story, where are you today? Are you . . .

○ Living a "Pardon me, Lord" life—struggling to believe that God has your back?
○ Spinning your wheels on a gravel road of self-sufficiency?
○ Looking for flames to shoot out of a rock as a sign that God is with you?

My "Pardon me" moment with God back in 1993 ended with the Holy Spirit pressing on my mind a wonderful idea to create exciting, fun events in all of our stores that helped generate the revenue we were depending on from Microsoft. It was a miracle—not as dramatic as fire consuming a sacrifice, but I will never forget it. And I have never doubted since that God has my back.

DAY 9

A BLIND SPOT

Not what we have but what we enjoy, constitutes our abundance.

EPICURUS

WE BOUGHT A NEW SUV last year that's more computer than automobile. It has a really neat feature: As you're driving, it can sense another vehicle coming up on its side. When the approaching car enters your blind spot, little lights flash on the side mirrors, indicating the potential for an accident if you were to change lanes. This fabulous technology is sure to prevent many accidents, but if only we had a similar innovation that could alert us to other hazard zones in our lives—specifically when jealousy and envy are pumping through our veins, racing toward our hearts.

Jealousy and her evil twin, Envy, are often the blind spots in our lives. Both are fueled by comparison, which is available to us 24-7 through every social media site. As a result, a shallow, incomplete, inconsequential opinion of ourselves lurks close behind, providing the perfect collision course to a sense of scarcity.

In his book *Respectable Sins: Confronting the Sins We Tolerate*, author Jerry Bridges points out two important distinctions of jealousy and envy that I think all women should hear. He says, "Sinful jealousy occurs . . . when we are afraid someone is going to become equal to or even superior to us."[4] I've never thought about jealousy in this well-articulated manner, but I can reflect on a time when I was a young professional and learned that an associate of mine was being considered for a promotion. Roaring up on one side was a really ugly car; the model was called Insecurity. On the other side, speeding out of nowhere, was the model Jealousy. We were on a spiritual collision course. Through prayer, I found God's grace and forgiveness and the filling of the Holy Spirit to replace my professional self-doubt with assurance in his timing and will.

When envy races up next to us—often out of the blue—some of us can't see where it came from. As Jerry Bridges explains, "We tend to envy those with whom we most closely identify . . . [and] we tend to envy in them the areas we value most."[5] Ouch. I'm sure I've been sideswiped by envy, too. As we consider the things we hold most dear, it's easy to see how the shiny new cars of Desire and Envy can cause a wreck on the highway to lasting peace. Prestige, advancement, friendships, community, loving relationships, and having children are just a few of the things many of us cherish, revere, or long for.

If you're not sure if you have a blind spot when it comes to jealousy and envy, here are some questions to honestly consider and pray over:

- Am I overly critical of someone? What's really behind this critical spirit of mine?
- Am I constantly comparing myself to others? Why do I feel a need to do that?
- Am I always competing with someone? What am I trying to prove?

JEALOUSY AND SELFISHNESS ARE NOT GOD'S KIND OF WISDOM. SUCH THINGS ARE EARTHLY, UNSPIRITUAL, AND DEMONIC. FOR WHEREVER THERE IS JEALOUSY AND SELFISH AMBITION, THERE YOU WILL FIND DISORDER AND EVIL OF EVERY KIND.

JAMES 3:15-16

Trusting God's will and provision for your life, rather than comparing it to others', turns on the blind spot indicator. But if you still continue to struggle with jealousy and envy, please commit another profound quote to memory: "If the grass is greener on the other side of the fence, you can bet the water bill is higher."

DAY 10

LET THE CREDITS ROLL

He who kneels the most stands best.

D. L. MOODY

OVER MY THIRTY-PLUS-YEAR career I have had the privilege of working alongside some incredibly talented individuals. Several were visionaries whose ideas blossomed into successful businesses. A few were highly creative people who could produce stimulating graphics and advertising campaigns. Some had been blessed with the phenomenal gift of producing annual sales in the seven- and eight-figure range. These people weren't just somewhat gifted in their respective fields; they were to their chosen crafts what Tom Hanks is to acting: blessed beyond measure. They made their roles look so easy.

Unfortunately, not all of them got to experience a happy ending to their movie. Many of them suffered repeated setbacks that upended their work and business relationships, resulting in their termination. How heartbreaking it is to watch so many talented stars fall to the earth over one common heart condition: pride.

The constricting process typically starts slow; it's subtle and often begins when the individual achieves considerable success in a particular role or project. The greater the success, the more likely the person comes to believe it is of his or her own making—taking the credit as theirs alone, not acknowledging others who gave great support to the overall work (one never gets to the top alone) or more importantly God, who blessed the person with his or her amazing talent in the first place! Once pride has settled into the deepest chambers of the heart, it becomes a most difficult task to remove.

Getting one's pride in check is a reflective, personal journey. It takes self-awareness to recognize this ugly condition for what it is and humility to help correct it, lest we crash and burn in our personal relationships and our professional careers. As we hold on to the rope of an inflated ego, we often find it begins to fray, impacting our work, marriage, parenting, friendships, and overall state of contentment. When we see our pride overriding our peace, it's time to let go and look to God to show us a better way. We can't be self-aggrandizing while embracing the abundant life, because humility is required for us to be taught, corrected, led, and counseled by God. And without humility, how do we ever receive his grace?

Consider these five statements as true or false as you assess your heart:

- I rarely ask God's guidance in my work or as I volunteer. I'm a pro.
- I talk over others because I am the expert. I often command more than I collaborate.
- I can't remember the last time I got down on my knees to humbly thank God for the talents he has blessed me with.
- I avoid giving credit to others for fear it will diminish me.
- I am frequently frustrated with others because they're not as smart or gifted as I am.

GOD OPPOSES THE PROUD BUT GIVES GRACE TO THE HUMBLE.
JAMES 4:6

Sometimes we're spread too thin because we think *everything* is about us. However, there's a great antidote for pride. Self-effacement is such a lovely attribute, especially when it gives credit to the one to whom credit is due. And adopting that attitude, sister, is something you *can* be proud of.

DAY 11

WHO'S FOR LUNCH?

If you haven't got anything nice to say about anybody, come sit next to me.
ALICE LONGWORTH

LAST WEEK I NOTICED two women sharing lunch. Their conversation started light and lively, but by the time their entrées were served, their bodies were leaning in over the table, their heads nearly touching, pupils dilated, and hands gesturing wildly. I don't know *what* they were talking about, but I'm pretty sure the topic didn't include a new recipe they had just tried or last Sunday's convicting sermon. Oh, no. These women were not talking about a "what" but a "who." The juiciest conversations are always about someone, rather than something, are they not? Unfortunately, gossip over lunch—or any other time—will affect the condition of your heart, spreading your sweet spirit too thin.

We have all been gossiped about. I've had unkind things said about me to others (just as you probably have as well). Whether those comments came from our girlfriends, family members, or coworkers, it is hurtful to know we were the subject of their critique and conversation.

But I have certainly made mistakes in this area too. My "sharing," which seemed to be so important or even justifiable in the moment, has never profited me. I'm sure I have hurt others with my opinions and observations. Though I've never knowingly lied about another person, spread a malicious rumor, or revealed a confidence, I've certainly expressed my feelings to others in ways that were less than edifying. Did those snarky remarks get back to the person about whom I spoke?

25

Of course they did. And as innocent as those words seemed in the moment, in the long run I felt like crap. That's how I know that gossip is something we can't continue to feast on if we want to claim our great inheritance of peace and abundance and joy.

Gossip can cultivate negativity where none previously existed. I've seen this happen at PTA, among soccer moms, in the workplace, and at Bible study. Yes! Even Bible study—maybe especially because it *is* Bible study—is a fertile soil for Satan to farm. He can drop a single seed of discontentment and will often get his desired results of complaining spirits or fractured relationships within weeks. What starts as a ninety-minute focus on God, his Word, and fellowship with other believers becomes something sad and sinful. Girlfriend, don't tell me Satan doesn't know what he's doing. We're being manipulated to live in a dry, deficient state of scarcity, and we're nuts to let it happen again and again and again.

If you're not quite sure if gossip is something you struggle with, ask yourself,

- When was the last time I said something untoward about someone to someone else?
- Would I be embarrassed if my boss, husband, friends, or family members knew what I said about them last week?
- Do I get a "rush" when I gossip or criticize others?
- Do I feel superior or smarter when I'm "critiquing" others?
- After gossiping about someone else, do I feel better or worse—or do I even acknowledge my cattiness?

THE TIME IS COMING WHEN EVERYTHING THAT IS COVERED UP WILL BE REVEALED, AND ALL THAT IS SECRET WILL BE MADE KNOWN TO ALL. WHATEVER YOU HAVE SAID IN THE DARK WILL BE HEARD IN THE LIGHT, AND WHAT YOU HAVE WHISPERED BEHIND CLOSED DOORS WILL BE SHOUTED FROM THE HOUSETOPS FOR ALL TO HEAR!

LUKE 12:2-3

Negative talk is a contributor to diluted living, but with God's grace, sister, we can overcome this hurtful habit. When you go out for lunch, commit to talking about something grand, life-giving, and honorable. You'll feel abundantly better than you might if you have to eat your words at a later date and time.

DAY 12

EXCESSIVE WORSHIP

One very difficult aspect about sin is that my sin never feels like sin to me.
My sin feels like life, plain and simple. My heart is an idol factory
and my mind an excuse-making factory.

ROSARIA BUTTERFIELD

WHEN I FIRST READ this quote by Rosaria Butterfield, I was immediately convicted. I'm not sure a clearer picture has been painted for us that relates to idol worship in the twenty-first century. Because none of us (I hope) bows down to a golden calf as the Israelites did in the Old Testament, I fear we often fail to recognize this heart condition of idol worship in our own selves because those things we worship look so much like normal life.

We let work and volunteer endeavors commandeer our mental, physical, and emotional faculties, becoming idols that require our constant attention. We obsess over food, eating either too much or not enough. We fixate on exercise, sacrificing other important pursuits and relationships to sculpt the perfect set of abs. We shop 'til we drop. We spend hours in stores or online, and if we don't buy that longed-for item, we dream about the day we will. We're addicted to our electronics. Most of us would freak out if our phones dropped in the water. I can't say many of us would have the same reaction if our Bibles fell in the pool. We parent according to the times: Our marriages and budgets are sacrificed for those cute kids we completely adore.

Who is missing in our idol factory? God. We rarely worship him to excess—like we do the latest fad diet, Facebook, or a new pair of heels—because we're worshiped out.

I live in a glass house, so I'm not throwing stones. But I'm sharing because this is something I struggle with too. I can make excuses all day long for the things I invest my time, energy, and money in that add not one ounce to a profoundly fruitful life. Yes, they're fun things and not necessarily wrong, but when service, prayer, worship, and monetary giving are marginalized for their sake, they have become our gods—and when this happens, we have to let them go.

Are you lacking an abundant life and lasting peace because trivial things, activities, or even people you love have become your gods? Consider these questions:

○ What percent of your time do you worship God? What percent of your time do you worship stuff?
○ What do you spend the majority of your time thinking about, strategizing about, or doing?
○ If God asked you to give up one thing, what is that one thing that you would struggle to sacrifice for him?

YOU MUST NOT HAVE ANY OTHER GOD BUT ME. YOU MUST NOT MAKE FOR YOURSELF AN IDOL OF ANY KIND OR AN IMAGE OF ANYTHING IN THE HEAVENS OR ON THE EARTH OR IN THE SEA. YOU MUST NOT BOW DOWN TO THEM OR WORSHIP THEM, FOR I, THE LORD YOUR GOD, AM A JEALOUS GOD WHO WILL NOT TOLERATE YOUR AFFECTION FOR ANY OTHER GODS.

EXODUS 20:3-5

It's an interesting time in which we live—a time when our lives are full of idols that we have made for ourselves and our families. We didn't carve them out of wood or cast them from silver or gold, but we have created them nonetheless.

DAY 13

BRAIN SURGERY
AND A HEART TRANSPLANT

God doesn't make orange juice. God makes oranges.
REVEREND JESSE JACKSON

LIFELESS. After speaking with some women of late, this single word seems to describe their marriages. Hearing stories ranging from struggles and hardship to boredom and apathy, I listened as these women shared how their commitment and love, now spread too thin, were struggling to gain victory over busy lifestyles and competing needs. Unsure of how to make things better, they let futility become the distant drumbeat by which they took steps toward the slow, quiet, and agonizingly lonely march to the end.

Is it our ill-informed illusions of a perfect union that hasten the destruction of what was once a beautiful, vibrant relationship, or is it the selfish way in which we often love? Who can save the marriage— a brain surgeon or a heart specialist? Based on the condition of most of the patients I've visited with, I think we need both. Stat.

Opting to invest in and reestablish a relationship that will be rooted in peace, contentment, and mutual respect is definitely a head thing. Likewise, we know there is a heart condition that must be addressed as well. While the heart must approach every relationship in humility, be willing to extend and receive forgiveness, and show gratefulness for what has been given, the mind must be equally committed and willing to do the hard work required to rebuild a relationship that has been neglected by frantic living and putting children first. (Lord, have mercy. If we let them, those little stinkers can pour the coolant on the steamiest of marriages.)

Like all couples, our daughter, Shauna, and son-in-law, Adam, have had their challenges. When they found themselves listening to the distant sound of a funeral march, they pulled themselves out of the pit of despair and opted to take action. Calling on the minister who married them, they asked for and received a copy of their wedding vows. That night, while sitting at their kitchen table, they recited each commitment, one by one. This time around, there was no flowered altar, no flickering candles, no beautiful white dress, no onlookers. Just the two of them with a tearstained piece of paper and a complete and palpable reliance on the grace and power of God to rescue their marriage.

> LOVE IS PATIENT AND KIND. LOVE IS NOT JEALOUS OR BOASTFUL
> OR PROUD OR RUDE. IT DOES NOT DEMAND ITS OWN WAY. IT IS
> NOT IRRITABLE, AND IT KEEPS NO RECORD OF BEING WRONGED. . . .
> LOVE NEVER GIVES UP, NEVER LOSES FAITH, IS ALWAYS HOPEFUL, AND
> ENDURES THROUGH EVERY CIRCUMSTANCE.
>
> 1 CORINTHIANS 13:4-7

If your marriage is spread too thin, would you and your mate prayerfully consider . . .

- Your priorities: Put God first, date night second (prioritize you as a couple), and, to ensure those sweet kids aren't drug along on that march with you, make them a loving but necessary third.
- Your perspective: You were actually made for God, not one another. Your mate will never be able to fulfill *all* your needs because he never was meant to.
- Your commitment: Love is as demanding as a newborn child. It cries—begs—to be fed and nurtured. Cherish the commitment you made to one another as you would a precious, helpless life.

- Your presence: Work and e-mail, social media and friends, and the constant distractions that are a part of parenthood all contribute to a lifeless, loveless relationship. Choose carefully what you allow to affect your marriage.

My first marriage failed, so I know what this drumbeat sounds like. Don't be resigned to the mind-set that it's over; don't pull the plug. Call the Great Physician who can heal both the head and the heart—then get to work.

DAY 14

WIND SHIFT

I've never been a millionaire but I just know I'd be darling at it.
DOROTHY PARKER

WE HAD SLEPT THROUGH THE STORM. The wind was blowing slightly from the south when we went to bed, but the cold front and accompanying lightning, thunder, and rain evidently arrived during the night. We would never have known about the storm, or that it was driven by a strong north wind, had we not noticed the huge potted plant that had toppled over in our courtyard.

As I was cleaning up the debris, I started to wonder how often I sleep through other storms in my life. Just like jealousy and envy, another condition of the heart that can lead to a sense of scarcity is greed. Rather than riding in on hurricane-force winds, greed is quite stealthy, arriving by a breeze that softly whispers, "I need . . . I want . . . I deserve . . . *more.*" This gentle breeze lulls us into a state of discontentment—and if we're not awakened to it, we might find ourselves gradually blown to a place where we'll never find the contentment Jesus promises.

So often we think of fictional characters like stingy ol' Ebenezer Scrooge when we think of greed. We associate the term with hoarding or keeping things for ourselves rather than being charitable toward others. But there is another side of greed to consider, a side that God warns us about: the hunger or longing for more of this world, rather than more of him. Failing to recognize or feel the wind shift, we awaken one day to find we've been blown into a twisted way of thinking. We resolve that to have the abundant life, we must strive for and amass more.

You might ask, isn't abundance about having more? If you look up the word in *Merriam-Webster*, you'll see that one definition is, in fact, "affluence and wealth," leading us to this justification: *Surely more money is good; think of all I could give away. More possessions would not be bad—I could open my home with its beautiful furnishings to welcome others. If I had more power and fame, I could better influence others for Christ.* These are all great ideas. However, if you had more, the question is what percentage of your wealth, possessions, time, and energy would you truly contribute? Five percent or one hundred percent? How much are you contributing now? The percentage would likely be the same.

Greed is the excessive desire for anything more than what we've already achieved or been given, which is the exact opposite of contentment and fulfillment. If we continually live and operate in a state of half-empty, our hearts will never find that place of overflowing fullness. Striving for "more" propels us toward a frantic life and prevents us from realizing this fabulous state of abundance that only Christ can offer. Instead of cashing in our promise of lasting peace, we put his offer off for another day, another month, another year, or a different life stage. But what if we don't get another day, month, or year? What if this is it? Will the "more" we're chasing ever be enough to bring us peace as we draw our last breath?

So, which way is your wind blowing?

- I just need more money.
- I just need more time.
- I just need more stuff.
- I just need more clothes.
- I just need to be more content with what I've been blessed with.

WATCH OUT! BE ON YOUR GUARD AGAINST ALL KINDS OF GREED; LIFE DOES NOT CONSIST IN AN ABUNDANCE OF POSSESSIONS.
LUKE 12:15, NIV

A good friend of mine, nearly twenty years my senior, shared with me that the older we get, the less we need. I hope it's because as we age, we finally begin to realize that in the end, he's *all* we need.

DON'T FLOCK YOUR TREE

You should not honor men more than truth.

PLATO

STEVE AND I ONCE LIVED on the sixteenth floor of a high-rise. With a striking view of downtown Dallas, we loved everything about our home except the rule prohibiting live Christmas trees, which were banned due to the potential fire hazard. So artificial tree shopping we went. After wandering the store for a good hour, Steve was thrilled when we finally decided on a prelit, majestic Fraser fir. What a beauty. She even had snow! Flocked to the nines, I must say that for a fake tree, she looked really good, even if she wasn't the real deal.

This fake Fraser fir might have been a good solution for having a Christmas tree that year, but to live an uncommon life of lasting peace, we have to be the real deal, and nowhere does it get more real than when our integrity is on the line. Simply stated: Lying by omission is deceptive. It's like "flocking" the truth.

Back in the late eighties as a twenty-eight-year-old inside sales associate, I was recruited by a technology distributor to lead a small team of sales and logistics managers who served their largest account. The management role called upon my strategic problem-solving skills, my ability to motivate and lead, and my love for serving clients. Every day I was doing what I did best. It was wonderful. That is, until the day I discovered that the owners of the company were defrauding my customer.

The first whiff that something was wrong came through a slip of the tongue by someone in accounting. My interest piqued, I began to research the situation quietly and soon came to the realization that what I thought was an honorable, respectable organization was, in fact, not. The situation was black and white, leading me to the conclusion that I could neither actively nor passively participate in such activity. But the dilemma was great: To expose the wrongdoing to the customer would result in them canceling their contract, putting my team and other people at the company I cared for out of work. Weeks of sleepless nights ensued as I wrestled with the dilemma, finally deciding to execute a quiet resignation. Rather than expose the truth to the customer, you might say that I "flocked my tree" as I gave them a vague excuse for my departure. Business continued as normal for both parties—for a few months. But God has a way of ensuring those of us who seek the abundant life have every opportunity to live it.

Valuing truth, not *a version* of the truth that has been covered up, God provided me with a chance meeting with my old customer, a few months after my departure. While sitting in his office, he asked me directly why I left my former employer. At that moment, I came face-to-face with honoring truth over man, and I exposed the fraud. The consequences were as dire as I had expected: The customer canceled the contract, and the distributor eventually closed.

Since that experience, I've noticed time and again that to live an uncommon life, we have to be the real deal—especially when our integrity is at stake. When we seek to live with excellence, we are required to operate at the highest standard—anything less than honorable fails our God and ourselves.

Consider these questions:

- Are you spread too thin because you struggle or are torn about a situation that places your integrity at risk?
- Are you willing to let God lead you to a place of truth telling?

HE GRANTS A TREASURE OF COMMON SENSE TO THE HONEST.
HE IS A SHIELD TO THOSE WHO WALK WITH INTEGRITY.
PROVERBS 2:7

What happened to my career after all of this? The customer who was being defrauded asked me to come work for them, and three years later, I had worked my way up to being vice president of a publicly traded enterprise. You can't make this stuff up. God rewards integrity with a bountiful life (*and* uninterrupted sleep).

DAY 16

YOUR WILL BE DONE

The will of God will never take you,
Where the Spirit of God cannot work through you,
Where the wisdom of God cannot teach you,
Where the army of God cannot protect you,
Where the hands of God cannot mold you.

UNKNOWN

ONE OF THE GREATEST difficulties Steve and I have experienced as parents was watching our son, Scott, get lost to the underworld of drugs. The struggle and fear we faced only escalated when he went missing. As any parent can imagine, at first I panicked. I called his friends, then friends of his friends, and eventually total strangers to try to locate him. As the days turned into weeks, then into months, and eventually years, Steve called the morgue on a monthly basis as I begged God to keep my son safe and bring him home alive.

Only by the grace of God did I weather this storm, and only by his exceptional mercy did I gain supernatural strength and lasting peace. By putting this situation and *the outcome* in the Lord's hands, I learned how to trust God in a way I had never been challenged to do so before. The day I prayed (and really meant it), "Your will be done" was a turning point for my faith (and my sanity). But these are hard words to pray, aren't they?

God's will. These two words strung together might be two of the most frightening words in the English language. For those of us who are control freaks, being malleable to God's divine plan for our work, relationships, marriages, and children can be a little mind-bending. We know what we *want*, but what if God doesn't want that for us? What if God's plan for us or someone we love involves challenges or even suffering in order to learn and grow? What if he deems a relationship—one that we want so badly—is not in our best interest? *Lord, have mercy*, we pray. *This is scary!*

Until it's not. I found when I was spread thin physically, emotionally, and spiritually by Scott's absence and walking through that dark night of desperation that it was a liberating release to give it all to God. In hindsight I can see his perfect timing and faithfulness and how things were resolved better than I could have hoped. When we give up the fight for our own way, we gain strength through prayer. During difficult situations our stamina is increased, our endurance is improved, and, as we gain power through him, we settle into that warm embrace of his peace.

YOUR WILL BE DONE.

MATTHEW 6:10

God's will for Scott was for him to return to us. There are no words to express that incredible day when he arrived home or to describe the joy in rebuilding our relationship over the past nine years—even on those days when life isn't perfect. But God's timing, the resulting faith lessons, and the experience of having a peace that passed all understanding throughout the crisis convinces me all the more that his plan was, and continues to be, absolutely divine.

A few questions for you, my friend:

- Do you resist praying, "Not what I want, Father, but what you desire for me and those I love"?
- Are you in the habit of rescinding your prayer of "Your will be done"?
- Are you ready to restore your joy and lasting peace by waiting for or adapting to his perfect plan?

It could be time to let go of the ropes of resistance with some rejoicing. It's rocket fuel for the extraordinary life when you finally trust that his will is the *only* way.

DAY 17

WAITING IN LINE

I am extraordinarily patient, provided I get my own way in the end.
MARGARET THATCHER

"I AM NOT WAITING IN THIS LINE." This is a common phrase I hear from Steve whenever there is a string of people standing at a window to buy tickets, a long list of diners waiting for a table, or a halt in traffic at the off-ramp of a particular exit. The man will drive five miles out of his way not to wait.

Unfortunately, as my grandmother would say, "This is the pot calling the kettle black." Girlfriend, patience is not my strong suit, either. I can go one better than the late prime minister Margaret Thatcher: I am extraordinarily patient, provided I get my own way right *now*!

Patience when waiting for an open table at a restaurant is one thing; being patient while waiting for God's divine plan to play out is something else. As you read yesterday, I completely trust that God's will is *the* way for me—I'd just like it now, please. I don't care to be left in a state of uncertainty or mystery; I want closure. I'm sure you can see how this attitude can sometimes be a barrier to living a joyful life because there are times when a resolution doesn't come for y . . . e . . . a . . . r . . . s. Ugh.

My greatest trial in having patience with God's divine plan was his timing during the years Scott was in and out of drug rehab and when he went missing. Night after night, day after day, I continued to trust God and his plan completely, but after a period of time I grew weary of waiting. I wanted answers. I wanted to know my son was alive and well. I wanted him to be healed of his addiction. But I knew my own efforts were futile; I had to pray and trust not only God's will but his timing. The waiting was not always joyful, but it was profitable because it afforded me time to develop the sweetest reliance on God I had ever known. The longer our saga played on, the more reliant I became on my God for his strength and the more I grew to trust his redemption of this situation.

What about you?

o Are you allowing your impatience with God's timing to eat away at and weaken your relationship with him, or are you trusting in his promises as nourishment for the abundant life?

o Are you willing to give up your timeline and find your rest in his?

o Will you come back and read this devotion a year from now? Two years from now? I'd be curious if God's timing wasn't just perfect.

I WAITED PATIENTLY FOR THE LORD TO HELP ME, AND HE TURNED TO ME AND HEARD MY CRY. HE LIFTED ME OUT OF THE PIT OF DESPAIR, OUT OF THE MUD AND THE MIRE. HE SET MY FEET ON SOLID GROUND AND STEADIED ME AS I WALKED ALONG. HE HAS GIVEN ME A NEW SONG TO SING, A HYMN OF PRAISE TO OUR GOD. MANY WILL SEE WHAT HE HAS DONE AND BE AMAZED. THEY WILL PUT THEIR TRUST IN THE LORD.

PSALM 40:1-3

As a side note, God's timing regarding Scott's return had little to do with me (beyond building my faith and reliance on him). God's perfect timing was all about Scott. My abundance was just a by-product of waiting in line for the blessing.

DAY 18

BACKING INTO A WALL

As the Hebrews were promised the land, but had to take it by force,
one town at a time, so we are promised the gift of self-control,
yet we also must take it by force.

EDWARD WELCH, *"Self-Control: The Battle against 'One More'"*

OUR SUV HAS ANOTHER cool feature: It is designed to assist me as I back out of a parking space or our driveway—and let me tell you, it's most effective. As soon as I put the vehicle in reverse, a series of beeps begins, pulsing faster and faster and louder and louder the closer I approach an obstacle. The system is obnoxious, but it works. I'd have to be asleep at the wheel to back into anything.

Having an active sense of self-control is like having parking assist for our thoughts, emotions, and behaviors. When we have a strong awareness of self, we have the internal warning systems and power we need to accelerate to an abundant life (rather than run over things).

Some people think of self-control as synonymous with physical self-discipline, which often leads to topics like eating or dieting. I have great self-restraint when it comes to sauerkraut; I struggle more with these little chocolate-covered graham crackers I recently found. Yum.

While self-control over our diets and exercise habits is important (even too much of a good thing can be too much and indicates an opportunity for self-restraint), it's the control we have over our feelings, emotions, and reactions that helps grease the slide to lasting peace. Instability, harsh reactions, and agitation—that's the stuff that has doomed many a career and relationship. Those who lack the ability to discern their physical and emotional drivers and objectively counter their desires often find themselves backed into a corner that might look like this:

- A sales executive driven by the need to be the top performer runs over others to get her deal. However, when the sales manager puts a kibosh on her actions, her agitation mounts, and she abruptly quits her job (with no other job prospects in sight and a family of five to help support).
- A buyer, with an uncontrollable need to fuel her status and power, successfully extorts her vendors for years, only to be finally exposed, fired from her position, and driven from her industry.
- A wife, lacking confidence and purpose, suspects her husband of cheating. The unfounded suspicions she allows to play through her head develop into distrust; her accusatory and critical tone eventually drives a wedge between her and her faithful spouse.

While a chocolate-covered graham cracker here and there will not bring about our destruction (praise the Lord!), the lack of discipline or desire to consciously discern our thoughts, desires, and motivations can. To critically evaluate our responses before we speak is a gift—one that has been given to us. But to use it, we have to unwrap it. Self-control is not something we can opt in and opt out of—we don't get to pick and choose where and when we activate "the assist."

Some of us recognize our "beeps," but others of us need a better warning system. Which one best describes your state of self-control?

- I am completely self-aware and able, through prayer, to self-edit and control my thoughts, words, and actions on the fly (and before they fly).
- I'm afraid I might lack discernment in the moment as to why I think and do some of the things I think and do.

- I know I struggle with self-control, but it's not my fault; other people drive me to react.

THE GRACE OF GOD HAS APPEARED THAT OFFERS SALVATION TO ALL PEOPLE. IT TEACHES US TO SAY "NO" TO UNGODLINESS AND WORLDLY PASSIONS, AND TO LIVE SELF-CONTROLLED, UPRIGHT AND GODLY LIVES IN THIS PRESENT AGE.

TITUS 2:11-12, NIV

Pray for strength and wisdom to exercise restraint. The extra-ordinary life is often realized by what you don't do.

DAY 19

POLLUTANTS

The mingled incentives which lead to action
are often too subtle and lie too deep for us to analyze.
JOHANN KASPAR LAVATER

IN THE HEAT OF SUMMER, hanging over our shiny city like Darth Vader's cape is a very dull, dirty film. As the heat builds, smog settles over us, giving us a visual to the air pollution that we daily live in and breathe. These gases that swirl invisibly around us contribute to ailments as minor as bronchitis (it's only minor if you're not the one with bronchitis) and illnesses as serious as emphysema.[6]

And much like these pollutants that so often go unnoticed, there's a form of contamination that settles over our own hearts that I'm afraid most of us fail to see. What clouds our success both at work and in our personal relationships is often the pollutant of impure motives.

When we fail to flourish in a particular area of our lives, we have to search our hearts to determine if a well-disguised agenda is to blame. The driving force behind our relationships, our desires, and sometimes even our business dealings isn't always easy to identify. It can even be imperceptible to the owner. But when relationships crumble, friendships suffer, or deals go sideways, the offender must search his or her heart.

Women must be vigilant against this pollutant because it is not God-honoring, and oftentimes other women can see an impure motive a mile away. Attending Bible study to build a network to sell more Mary Kay? Going to church to promote your real estate practice? Purposely exposing an error to undermine a colleague and make yourself look better? Sisters, we have to be on guard as to the "why" behind our actions. Satan often takes this easily disguisable human failing and uses it to diminish our success at work, hurt our reputations with our friends and peers, and devalue our positions within our families. Satan will disguise these actions as just.

It's heart examination time:

- Do you consciously question the motivation behind some of your actions?
- When you identify an impure motive, do you ignore it and move forward or call yourself out and change your actions?
- Do you consider yourself more pure than you really are?

WE CAN MAKE OUR OWN PLANS, BUT THE LORD GIVES THE RIGHT ANSWER. PEOPLE MAY BE PURE IN THEIR OWN EYES, BUT THE LORD EXAMINES THEIR MOTIVES. COMMIT YOUR ACTIONS TO THE LORD, AND YOUR PLANS WILL SUCCEED.

PROVERBS 16:1-3

How do I know this topic so well? I have caught myself on more than one occasion sporting a black cape, and it wasn't Chanel. And it wasn't pretty.

DAY 20

NO PAIN. NO GAIN.

I am so clever that sometimes I don't understand a single word of what I am saying.
OSCAR WILDE

"No PAIN, NO GAIN" is a common expression among athletes. If I've heard my Steve quote it to me once, I've heard it a hundred times as he "encourages" me to push harder through a series of sit-ups and planks. I can be holding a perfect plank position until I tremble, and he'll continue to encourage me to improve my form. Any thoughts of shortcuts and idleness, as tempting as they are, must go by the wayside because they work against the desired outcome—abs of steel.

Our shortcuts can work against us, too, as we strive to journey toward the abundant path. "What?" you ask. "Idleness? Laziness? Us? No way! We're hyperactive, overachieving, work-our-fannies-off Americans." Yes, ma'am, we are. That's what tempts us to take those time-saving routes that can bankrupt us both literally and figuratively.

My first professional shortcut came in the early 1990s. I had carefully negotiated a contract with a major supplier and given them my word that I would use the additional profits secured in the negotiation to fund marketing activities that would benefit both organizations. The following week, our executive staff decided that we would get out in front of a new competitor by placing an ad (that included products from this supplier) to drive our sales. The problem was, we (the merchant staff) had only a short time to provide the product information and pricing to our advertising department for ad layout, a process that would take hours.

But lucky me, I had a shortcut! I had previously built a comprehensive spreadsheet with this particular supplier's products that listed both our negotiated cost and the retail price. I simply handed over the spreadsheet with this detailed instruction: Please use the retail price. I felt so smart for having already created this time-saving document, I simply amazed myself! And I amazed our executives and the supplier when the ad broke a day later advertising the *cost* of the product, not the retail price—a blatant violation of our contract.

When I realized what had happened, I *sprinted* (in my pencil skirt and stilettos, with my 90s permed tresses trailing behind me) to my boss's office. With a trembling voice, I explained what had happened as I watched his face go pale. He left me standing in his office, with tears pooling in my eyes, to gather the other executives. As I quickly assessed the situation, I knew the error was clearly mine; I should have never provided a file to our production staff that contained our cost in the first place. I should have taken the time to recreate the file. This wasn't a small mistake. This was a firing offense.

Within the hour, phone calls were made and apologies were extended to our supplier. I even got on a plane to meet the CEO of the offended company in an airport (between his connecting flights) to apologize in person. What did I say to him by way of an explanation? "I learned a really important lesson: My shortcut of delivering a prepopulated file, rather than investing the time to build a custom file, was costly and devastating for us all."

Oh, sister, learn from my mistake. Before the hard, cold reality of your own shortcuts hits you in the face, ask yourself,

- Am I trying to be so efficient that I'm putting my work, my customer, or my company at risk?
- Am I trying to shortcut a process in order to drive my own agenda?
- Am I being lazy?

GOOD PLANNING AND HARD WORK LEAD TO PROSPERITY, BUT
HASTY SHORTCUTS LEAD TO POVERTY.

PROVERBS 21:5

The story ends with grace. I wasn't fired (but deserved to be), and
the supplier didn't pull his contract (which he could have). I also learned
that laziness often cloaks herself in something we call a shortcut.

DAY 21

WORD PRUNING

Saint: A dead sinner revised and edited.

AMBROSE BIERCE

SOMETIMES PEOPLE DON'T UNDERSTAND A THING WE'RE SAYING. And yes, this includes our own families! Oh, they hear or read the words we send out into space, but they muffle the meaning; they take away something completely different from what we intended. Because communicating well with our loved ones and colleagues is key to successful relationships, both professional and personal, it's important that we welcome and, when appropriate, allow edits.

People often ask me if I find it difficult to write books, and I tell them, "Not really." Before sitting down at my computer or writing a single word on a page, I spend time in God's Word and in prayer. So, no—the words and stories just sort of flow, and I try not to get in the way of what God wants to say through my experiences and work. But going through the editing process is like having open-heart surgery without anesthesia. It hurts like crazy, and I think, *Will this ever end?* As I read over my editors' comments, I ask myself, *How do they not understand what I'm trying to communicate?* It seems perfectly clear to me! But the editing process is not about me. It's about you, the reader. My sweet (yes, they are adorable) editors ensure the clarity of my message to you.

The process has me thinking that we all could use some editing when it comes to conversations at work or with family members, because both our words and our tone can be completely taken out of context. This happened to me last week.

A concern regarding a segment of our business that I felt was going unaddressed had colored my inflection with one of my direct reports. My frustration over this issue surfaced in several meetings throughout the week. Although I thought I had been perfectly clear regarding my expectations and displeasure with this process, he read something altogether different from my comments and tone. I was unhappy with the project; he thought I was unhappy with him. I needed an editor.

Editors are those individuals God has blessed you with who will speak the truth in love to you. Editors are those who care deeply about your relationship or work and will invest in you to bring clarity to your writing and communication. Editors, too, can unintentionally encroach on your voice or your message, so pray for clarity and diplomacy should you need to stand firm. But be humble to accept when you're wrong or when the intent behind your words is unclear.

DEAR BROTHERS AND SISTERS, IF I SHOULD COME TO YOU SPEAKING IN AN UNKNOWN LANGUAGE, HOW WOULD THAT HELP YOU? BUT IF I BRING YOU A REVELATION OR SOME SPECIAL KNOWLEDGE OR PROPHECY OR TEACHING, THAT WILL BE HELPFUL. EVEN LIFELESS INSTRUMENTS LIKE THE FLUTE OR THE HARP MUST PLAY THE NOTES CLEARLY, OR NO ONE WILL RECOGNIZE THE MELODY. AND IF THE BUGLER DOESN'T SOUND A CLEAR CALL, HOW WILL THE SOLDIERS KNOW THEY ARE BEING CALLED TO BATTLE?

1 CORINTHIANS 14:6-8

Some questions for you today:

o Do you often have communication snafus?
o Have you asked a nonbiased third party to objectively weigh in on your communication style or choice of words?
o Do you often edit others without allowing this pruning for yourself?

Everything we say and *how* we say it matters. Ask God to bring you a good editor. He certainly brought one to me!

DAY 22

PASIÓN

My mission in life is not merely to survive, but to thrive;
and to do so with some passion, some compassion, some humor, and some style.
MAYA ANGELOU

ON OUR TRIP TO San Miguel de Allende, Steve and I elected to take a couple of tours arranged by the hotel. The *momento* we stepped into the SUV for our first excursion, we were welcomed by Mario, a warm and lively tour guide—and before we made it through the twisty streets of San Miguel to the freeway, we knew we were in the presence of a Mexican treasure.

Not only was Mario an expert in his native country's history and the surrounding area, he was the most passionate, expressive, happy, fulfilled professional I'd ever encountered in my life. Over the next two days, as we toured various UNESCO World Heritage Sites, we got to know this man of great faith.

We came to learn that although Mario drove a beautiful brand-new SUV, he didn't own it—or any other car for that matter. He took the bus to work every morning, leaving home very early. He shared with us details of his humble family life: the hopes he had for his daughter as she started college at the local university, and the challenges he faced motivating a teenage son. (Ha! We have more in common than what separates us!) His enthusiasm for his family, faith, work, city, and country was infectious. As we drove through the mountains of central Mexico, we got to see up close and personal what a bountiful life looks like when we embrace with a grateful heart just *whom* we work for:

Mario worked for his boss. This was not his car or his tour company. He was thankful for his job and the work that he felt *privileged* to perform each day.

Mario worked those two days for us. He went the extra mile to delight us, his customers, providing us a unique experience aligned with our personal interests.

Most importantly, Mario worked for the Lord. He gave everything he had in the form of passion, humor, and a *whole lot of style* over those two days, and I have no doubt God was glorified and well pleased with his faithful servant.

If asked, what would your customers, family members, fellow volunteers, or coworkers say about your service?

- Are you passionate about your work in order to best serve those you're working with and for?
- If you are, do you express your enthusiasm? Do your coworkers, boss, and customers benefit from your positive energy and joy?
- If not, what steps might you take to kindle that passion?
- Lastly, what do others hear you say about your work—especially your children?

WORK WITH ENTHUSIASM, AS THOUGH YOU WERE WORKING FOR THE LORD RATHER THAN FOR PEOPLE.
EPHESIANS 6:7

Mario was a witness to me, convicting me of my need to remember for whom I'm really working. And then to show it with all the gusto I can muster.

DAY 23

NOT SO PLAIN AFTER ALL

If you find yourself constantly trying to prove your worth to someone,
you have already forgotten your value.

UNKNOWN

A PLAIN WHITE BOWL SAT on a New York family's mantelpiece for years. Having purchased it at a garage sale for three dollars, the owners eventually became curious as to whether the bowl might have any value. After consulting with experts, it was confirmed: The plain white bowl was actually a Northern Song dynasty bowl, known as a Ding bowl, dating back to the tenth or eleventh century. The true value of the small vessel? Sotheby's sold the piece for 2.2 million dollars at auction.[7]

And just like this treasure, the sad reality for many of us women is our failure to realize our actual worth. We treat our lives, expend our time and resources, and listen to negative self-talk as if we're garage-sale castoffs. We think of ourselves as not pretty enough, smart enough, kind enough, funny enough, or talented enough. We discount our relationships and the impact we have on others. For all of us who have allowed our hearts to be conditioned by this mind-set, we need to do some investigation and research of our own. It would be a sin not to understand how truly priceless we are.

A huge deposit was paid for you and me. God sent his Son from heaven to live a difficult thirty-three years on earth as one of us. God developed the payment plan that Jesus was required to fulfill. Christ loved us so much that he made the final balloon payment on our behalf in the form of not just his death, but a torturous crucifixion. His payment was to ensure for us an abundant life of peace and joy on earth and an eternity spent with him. Knowing this, do you see just how extravagant you are? Can you imagine someone at Sotheby's trying to write your marketing copy? Here's what I imagine.

Loved from the beginning of time. Forgiven for every sin. Exhibits peace, joy, and comfort during the hardest of circumstances. Has trusted the Lord with all her prayers and petitions. Will spend eternity with God himself. We'll open the bid at . . .

It would be a shame to live one more hour unaware of your value. Consider these questions:

- Do you recognize you are a rare treasure?
- Do you understand the price that was paid for you?
- Can you see yourself as he sees you, rather than how you see yourself?
- Will you choose to live as the rare treasure that you are?

You were bought with a price; therefore glorify God in your body.

1 CORINTHIANS 6:20, NRSV

That grace extended to us wasn't cheap, and we're anything but plain. It's time we all show up to the abundant life and live like the precious, invaluable souls we are.

DAY 24

KUMBAYA

Tenderness and kindness are not signs of weakness and despair,
but manifestations of strength and resolution.

KAHLIL GIBRAN

NICE *AND* EFFECTIVE. Sounds like a tagline for bathroom tissue. But actually these words are a good summation for living the abundant life—especially for those of us in positions of leadership. Whether in our families, at work, at church, or in the places we serve as volunteers, being demanding and dismissive toward others (to get done what needs to get done) is easy and can be effective for a while, but it will likely contribute to an existence of scarcity.

Some of us realized we were leaders in the first grade as we ran to the front of the single-file line. But if you're like me, you may not have set out to be a leader; it just sort of happened one activity at a time, starting with organizing a group of classmates to take on cleaning the erasers. Subconsciously, some of us take on the roles of director, conductor, or chief, while others of us who have been perfectly happy to follow wake up one day to find that we have been appointed as the person in charge. Wide-eyed and knees knocking, we stand before a group of people who expect to be motivated and inspired. *Oh, good grief,* we think. *How did I get here?* Born leader or not, the demands of leadership can spread us too thin.

Not always, but often, for a group to be effective, the leader needs to be directive. We must be clear. We must be correct. We must drive efforts and tactics forward to achieve the objective. And it's here, when goals are not being met, that we resort to leading aggressively. I can tell you, firsthand, this does not work. Oh, I've realized short-term results, for sure, but they never stuck because the team was producing from a place of anxiety and fear of failure. Not until I adopted a more kumbaya management style did I feel I could lead *and* enjoy the abundant life.

If you were ever a Girl Scout, on a mission trip, or on a sports team of any type, there's a good chance you grew up singing the 1920s spiritual that became the theme song for campers throughout the ages. The word *kumbaya* is from the creole language Gullah, and it simply appeals to God to "come by here." The melody and deep meaning of the word are moving regardless of whether it's sung around the most beautiful campfire high in the woods or on a stinky school bus heading home from a volleyball tournament. *Come by here, my Lord* may be one of the finest concise expressions of wisdom, humility, hope, and kindness. You don't have to sing it—but to lead in a manner that is kind and productive, you do have to live it. *Come by here, my Lord,* when brought to the conference table or the kitchen table, expresses our own deficiencies and our dependence on God while exposing our faith through his divine intervention. It shows our compassion and concern for those around us.

In the workplace, on committees, and in our homes, we need the wisdom and humility expressed in this classic. Many a career gal has put on her mask of toughness to hold her own with the boys, to keep her direct reports in line, or to pave her way to the corner office, but in the process has failed to properly share her common frailty—her fears, her weaknesses, her humanness—with those she serves.

A life of lasting peace is rich in these moments, where authenticity, grace, and respect abound.

- Have you had a kumbaya moment with your teammates, subordinates, committee, or family members?
- What prevents you from exposing your faith, compassion, and humility to others?
- Is being the "tough" boss spreading you too thin?

WHEN SHE SPEAKS, HER WORDS ARE WISE, AND SHE GIVES
INSTRUCTIONS WITH KINDNESS.

PROVERBS 31:26

Strength and kindness are not mutually exclusive. Kumbaya.

DAY 25

WHAT'S ON YOUR HEART?

I DOUBT MANY PEOPLE WAKE UP each morning planning to sin. We just don't open our eyes and think, *Oh! Today I will be arrogant, prideful, and lustful. And maybe I'll do some gossiping, too.* But neither, unfortunately, do we open our eyes each morning and pray for a virtuous heart. And that's how sin so easily dilutes our lives, spreading our joy and fruitfulness too thin.

Before we can continue to address those things that negatively and positively impact our day-to-day lives—such as the quality of our thoughts, the discernment of our activities, and the pursuit of soul-searching for the truth, we must complete the conditioning of our hearts.

Consider these questions as we wrap up this first section:

- Did you identify the sins that so easily deplete you?
- Did you choose to pray for the power to overcome them? Good news! The victory is found in Christ, not yourself.
- Will you pursue the more virtuous path as a route to opt out of frantic living and opt in to lasting peace?
- Will you pray for the power to focus and act on the more bountiful, profitable virtues to claim the inheritance of the abundant life that has been promised to you?

ABBA FATHER,

We come to you completely overwhelmed by your love for us. We long to live a life that is uncommon—one that is honoring and pleasing to you.

We confess that we are often overwhelmed with the pace and flurry and sometimes the negativity in our lives. We are convicted of the sins of bitterness, envy, pride, anger, deception, and greed and pray that you will help us replace them with a spirit of forgiveness, appreciation, humility, patience, integrity, and charity. We seek to turn our gossip into words that lift up and build up and to speak with truth-bearing kindness. We lay down our extravagance and vanity and all of our idols to worship only you.

We come into your presence like the boy with the backpack, on our knees and overwhelmed with gratitude that you would give your Son to die for our sins, that you would seek to commune with us through your Word and guide and comfort us through a relationship developed in prayer. We thank you for being accessible to us every minute of every day.

We ask that you will give us a yearning and deep desire to live abundantly and replace the sins that so easily fan the fire of scarcity with the virtues that pave the way for a life lived with excellence—a life of joy and purpose and passion—drawing on your truth and wisdom. Equip us as we go through our days with deeper gratitude, greater self-control, and more powerful prayer.

We pray completely overwhelmed by the grace of your Son, Jesus Christ. Amen.

PART 2

MIND GAMES *You Can* WIN

DAY 26

RETHINK EVERYTHING

If you want things to be different,
perhaps the answer is to become different yourself.
NORMAN VINCENT PEALE

MANY TALENTED WOMEN have failed to realize their full potential as God intended. Not because of something they did or didn't do, but often because of what they were taught or what *they taught themselves* to think. Some gals who are spread too thin are not taxed by their schedule or the demands of their family and workplace, but are overwhelmed with negative self-esteem that has warped their beliefs and self-image. James 4:1 says, "What causes fights and quarrels among you? Don't they come from your desires that battle within you?"[8] Oh yes, James—we are often our own worst enemy.

Some of this negativity and doubt in our self-worth is the result of living in a very flawed world. Our culture has a way of sneaking into our psyches via movies, music, books, fashion, and trends, transporting us from a place of self-doubt to a land of self-loathing. I'll go out on a limb here and tell you that I believe Satan has his hooks set in us too. If he can convince us that an exhausting life is all we should hope for and attain, he's done his job for the day. Keeping us busy to the point that we're physically, mentally, and emotionally bankrupt is one thing, but playing mind games with us—well, that's a whole new ball game. To purposefully pursue the abundant life and lasting peace, we have to be willing to rethink everything we know.

I began taking piano lessons when I was five. By the time I was fifteen, I had developed some poor habits and techniques that I unwittingly picked up from a few of my various teachers. Over the next eight years, I was privileged to study with four different advanced instructors—sometimes three in the same semester—who set me straight. But it wasn't easy. I had to study, adopt new works into my daily practice, and establish new patterns of practicing. I was repeatedly critiqued and corrected, and I had to completely rethink the basics—going back to the beginning and playing scales! (I thought I'd die.)

To live an uncommon life, we must completely retrain our minds, replacing poor and even inaccurate thoughts with correct thinking, based on God's Word. Sometimes just being reminded of his truth will do the trick, but often we have to invest time and energy in repairing our flawed views. When we're willing, our blemished, unhealthy, and unguarded attitudes can be replaced with character and perspective that is both God- and self-honoring. After all, Christ sees you as a beautiful, treasured child without flaw.

Tell me, sister:

○ Do you sometimes feel like you're your own worst enemy?
○ Are you ready to replace errant thought with God's truth?

DO NOT REMEMBER THE FORMER THINGS, OR CONSIDER THE THINGS OF OLD. I AM ABOUT TO DO A NEW THING; NOW IT SPRINGS FORTH, DO YOU NOT PERCEIVE IT?
ISAIAH 43:18-19, NRSV

Too often we're lost in mind games that we never win. But be encouraged; there's a way out—a way toward victory. You'll need to learn a few rules along the way. But full disclosure: This is not like playing Go Fish, where you all of a sudden win. This is more like playing Axis & Allies. This game takes time, effort, and patience. It's a process that goes on forever.

YOU AREN'T WHO YOU THINK YOU ARE

The truth is beautiful, like you. The truth is you have been made perfect and are wholly loved. Chosen simply because you breathe, because you exist, because of who created you.

RACHELLE DEKKER, *The Choosing*

WHILE I WAS WRITING THIS BOOK, Steve and I took a brief break from our busy lives to vacation in Barcelona. Our hotel was located on the famous Passeig de Gràcia, which is lined with beautiful shops and restaurants and the most ornate buildings you can imagine—most dating back to the late 1800s to early 1900s. Barcelona is considered one of the most walkable cities in the world, and even part of this famous boulevard is closed to vehicle traffic. From midmorning to midnight, we noticed hundreds upon hundreds of people traversing this street to shop, eat, talk, and laugh. Some were strolling arm in arm, others hurrying. All carefully stepped around the beggar.

During our weeklong visit, we passed this man at least twice a day. We couldn't determine his age or his race, as he knelt on the ground with his elbows stationed firmly on the concrete and his head tucked between them as he held up a paper cup. He appeared more like a statue than a human, for he never moved.

My first sighting of him caught me by such surprise I didn't know what to make of him. Those of us who live in cities almost daily encounter homeless people asking for charity. But this man was different. He didn't have a sign, nor did he attempt to make eye contact.

All I could discern over a week of passing by to and fro was that he believed this was his station. At one point I thought I could hear God whisper, "I made you for more than this." And then I wondered if God was speaking to me or him. I could see so clearly how this child of God was living a life of scarcity—not because of his meager possessions or the few euro coins in his paper cup, but because he had accepted this station as his calling. Likewise, I see how easily our own self-devaluation can affect our purpose, our witness, and the life we're called to live abundantly, and it is here where the mind games begin.

Not only must we embrace that we are daughters of a heavenly King, we must learn to recognize and value our intellect, identify the attributes of our personalities that make us successful, and embrace our God-given talents. Suffering from an under- or overactive imagination is like starving when the pantry is fully stocked. We waste our lives in a virtual bent-over position, spread too thin by our own devaluation, and yet abundance is ours if we'll only stand up and receive it.

Do you often operate in a state of low self-worth or discounted value? Answer for yourself these questions:

○ Do I allow myself to consistently suffer from an overactive imagination that is clearly in conflict with God's holy Word and promise?
○ Do I easily accept compliments or notes of congratulations for a job well done from my boss or peers, or do I quickly discount my achievement?
○ Do I claim my identity as a daughter of the holy King?
○ Am I living with my head down or my head up?

YOU ARE A CHOSEN RACE, A ROYAL PRIESTHOOD, A HOLY NATION, GOD'S OWN PEOPLE.
1 PETER 2:9, NRSV

When we live a life of abundance, we have no doubt who made us, and we celebrate and embrace the way we were made. Don't let anyone, especially Satan, trick you into thinking anything else because *you* were definitely designed for something awesome. Look up—you're royalty.

DAY 28

BE A BLESSING

God doesn't bless us just to make us happy; He blesses us to make us a blessing.
WARREN W. WIERSBE

HAVING ACCUMULATED credit card points for years, Steve and I splurged and cashed them in for business-class seats for our trip to Barcelona. Playing with the reclining seats (on a Boeing 777 these puppies completely stretch out to make a bed!), dialing down the lighting, and tuning in to a favorite movie, I was as giddy as a high school girl on prom night. But coming home was a little different. Unable to reserve adjoining seats, Steve and I were separated, rows apart. Our glamorous jet for the return flight turned out to be a lesser plane, but still, we were in business class.

As I approached my seat, I recognized my seatmate as the person who had blatantly cut me off in line as we boarded the plane. I smiled and greeted her; her brief response was followed by a lengthy rant about the airline. It seems that she had purchased a first-class ticket for which there were no first-class seats, leaving her stuck in business class (with me as her seatmate). She went on to complain about the poor service extended by the flight attendants, the lack of communication and flight-status updates by the captain, and the movie selection. Some of her observations were correct, but I kid you not, there had to be at least twenty-five movies to choose from. But that really wasn't the point. The issue was the luxury accommodations failed to deliver to her expectations. She was not "blessed" in the manner she believed she deserved.

A couple of hours into the flight, I pulled out my computer and began working on one of my books. After a while she seemed intrigued and asked me what I did for a living. I told her that professionally I worked in a marketing capacity but that my passion was writing Christian devotionals for women. She blinked and responded with "Oh." I smiled and returned to my writing. Needless to say, this put a quick kibosh on our neighborly chat. As the flight continued through the meal service (I was served grilled salmon, rice, and snow peas that were awesome!), I decided to be a blessing to this woman no matter what she did or said. For every negative comment, I responded with a positive. With every critique of an individual, I offered a compliment. I was determined not to let her disappointment and expectation of receiving blessing after perfect blessing affect my hope of being one to her.

This is a mind game we all can win when we don't allow others to suck us into their negativity. Shifting our expectations from what we desire or deserve to what we can extend and exalt turns our anticipation from being blessed to being the one who blesses. By the end of our flight, my seatmate and I had become chummy. She had more questions about my books and beliefs. As we parted, I wished her well and could hear the surprise in her voice when she said, "You are so kind." Well dressed and attractive, she had no doubt as she boarded the plane that she was important. God provided me a divinely appointed seatmate to prove to her she was right.

So today and tomorrow and the day after tomorrow, will you . . .

- ○ Set out to be blessed or to be a blessing?

I AM GIVING YOU A NEW COMMANDMENT: LOVE EACH OTHER. JUST AS I HAVE LOVED YOU, YOU SHOULD LOVE EACH OTHER. YOUR LOVE FOR ONE ANOTHER WILL PROVE TO THE WORLD THAT YOU ARE MY DISCIPLES.
JOHN 13:34-35

I can tell you firsthand, extending the blessing, rather than being the recipient, will never leave you with missed expectations.

DAY 29

SINGING THE BLUES

Enjoy the little things, for one day you may look back
and realize they were the big things.
ROBERT BRAULT

OF ALL THINGS, I'm most ashamed to share with you that on any given day you might find me "singing the blues." Something as benign as having to run an errand during rush hour can turn my "head tune" of "Joyful, Joyful, We Adore Thee" to B. B. King's "The Thrill Is Gone." I can tell you straight up, singing the blues spreads me too thin.

Shifting our hearts, minds, and attitudes from a state of lament to a posture of acknowledgment and gratitude can have a profound effect on keeping us from a state of scarcity. The good news is that it only takes a wee bit of creativity and zero vocal ability. Our playlist must include all of the little (and sometimes mundane) things in our lives—and to see them as the blessings they are, we must turn off the blues.

To replace the frustrating tune of a three-year-old who refuses to stay in his bed, we must consciously acknowledge, at that moment, that women around the world are awake tonight, crying because they are barren. We must turn that dial to a song of gratitude that we've been blessed with a beautiful child. Instead of complaining about the weekly grocery run, we must acknowledge that there are women just a few miles away plucking a can of corn and day-old bread off the shelf at a food pantry. We must turn that dial to a song of gratefulness that we have a grocery store, with abounding options, to shop in and money in our handbags to pay for it. Looking at that mound of laundry—instead of belting out the never-ending laundry blues, we must acknowledge that most of us have appliances in our homes that do 95 percent of the work! When our professional work gets difficult—and when is it not?—we are often tempted to wail about the demanding expectations of the job. Acknowledging that there are thousands of people out of work or underemployed makes it easier to tune into the airwaves of thankfulness, remembering how fortunate we are not just to have *a* job—but *this* job.

After we sing a few rounds of "Kumbaya" as we did on day 24, our last song selection might be a song of thanksgiving or all five stanzas of "Amazing Grace," sung with a spirit of complete awe and recognition—which I think is probably the secret sauce of living the abundant life. If I could will every woman on the face of this earth a grateful spirit, I would. But I can't; nor are there words I can use to guilt anyone into a heart and mind of thankfulness. This is a *place* we all have to make our way to, but be assured, once we have settled our roots completely, we will never operate from a sad state of scarcity again.

You might have some blues playing in your head—most of us do. Write yours down, and look for the melody that might serve as an antidote. Start with the five things that have you spread thin today:

1._____

2._____

3._____

4._____

5._____

THE LORD IS MY STRENGTH AND SHIELD. I TRUST HIM WITH ALL MY HEART. HE HELPS ME, AND MY HEART IS FILLED WITH JOY. I BURST OUT IN SONGS OF THANKSGIVING.

PSALM 28:7

Gratitude—not talent, money, prestige, or any other thing we might hope for—can do the most for resetting the mind, heart, and soul toward abundant living. This life on earth is temporary. It can be good and full and wonderful, or it can be a whip. Resurrect your rejoicing. Get out your dancing shoes, and turn your dial to a happier song.

DAY 30

RETHINKING YOUR PURPOSE

I'm not anxious about my purpose in life because I only want to do God's will.
BROTHER LAWRENCE, *The Practice of the Presence of God*

ONE DAY I WAS VISITING with a dear friend of mine, discussing her very busy and, as it appears to me, incredibly rich and rewarding life. She is extremely successful, has a wonderful husband and multiple gorgeous homes, and is a devout Christian whose faith has been tested and refined over the years. But as she approached another birthday nearing her seventh decade, she began talking about her remaining time on earth. She asked me, "Is this really it? Is this all there is? Is this *really* what I'm supposed to be doing right now?" I understood her questions and concern. I've had this same conversation with women of all ages. Everyone wants to know the greater purpose for their being and what they are meant to accomplish in their time on earth.

For several years, I was fixated on this topic myself. Although I enjoyed a professional career, cared for my family, and volunteered for ministry and social programs that served the needy, I felt as though my contributions were shallow. Surely I was designed for more! But what did God need or want from me? Did he want me to be more deeply engaged? Did he want me to change my lifestyle? I prayed, asking God for direction. And then it came to me: My purpose wasn't to take on more responsibility or another volunteer role. My purpose was to love him. *Really* love him.

Since then I've learned that everything we do should be for the ultimate glorification of God, making our purpose here on earth not about us but all about him. Ellen—are you saying going to the office, sitting in a cubicle, and doing my mundane work is my purpose? When you do it for his glory and not your own, then absolutely! Carpooling kids, doing twenty loads of laundry a week, and wiping noses is my purpose? Yes, ma'am—when you do it out of love for your God.

But get sucked in by the deceitful mind game of "There's more to life than this," and we will stray from living righteous lives filled with "love, joy, peace, patience, kindness, goodness, faithfulness, gentleness, and self-control."[9] We can't fulfill our purpose when we are discontent because God cannot manifest his glory through us if we're held hostage by the world and a restless spirit.

We know our purpose must be something complex, deep, and amazing. And it is, but it is also simple: Our purpose is to love God with everything in our being.

As you think about your purpose,

- Have you been chasing a dream to make a contribution that glorifies you or God?
- Have you ever thought that the one and only reason you're on this earth is to love God?
- Do you see how sin and living a life of discontentment prevent you from fulfilling your ultimate purpose?

LOVE THE LORD YOUR GOD WITH ALL YOUR HEART, ALL YOUR SOUL, AND ALL YOUR STRENGTH.
DEUTERONOMY 6:5

Some people are called to teach, while others are meant to climb telephone poles. Some people are called to ministry, and some are called to collect trash. A friend of mine was called to heal; I was called to marketing. But our true purpose is all the same: to love and glorify God with everything we do. Isn't it nice to know there really is more?

DAY 31

FREEDOM OVER FOMO

He who has overcome his fears will truly be free.

ARISTOTLE

HAVE YOU HEARD about a "new" affliction being written about today? It's called FOMO—the fear of missing out—but it's hardly new. This feeling has been driving women to a state of frantic living for generations. Just watch a woman mention to her girlfriends over lunch that she found a great pair of shoes on sale, and you'll need to wipe the FOMO up off the table with a napkin. Like these ladies, I, too, am desperate to get to the Nordstrom sale rack. But a shoe sale isn't the only thing that will cause FOMO to play mind games with us.

Some of us fear that we'll be left behind because we feel we don't measure up. We operate as if we are incomplete or deficient, believing that others are outperforming us, outearning us, outpurchasing us, out-traveling us, and outliving us. We fear we're missing out on something that someone else has gained, and we end up anxious and unhappy. I can't prove it, but I'm almost certain that living a profoundly gratifying life and FOMO are incompatible.

While I was building my career and establishing my professional reputation in the technology industry, I was often driven by a state of fear. I was afraid I would fail to fulfill my potential. Frightened that any mistake I made would expose my company and/or me, I feared greatly that each day in the office could be my last. I was in my early thirties and had been afforded a great deal of responsibility and trust for my work experience and age. For nearly five years, I surfed on the waves of my company's success—some days hanging ten but other days wiping out mentally, emotionally, and physically. No, I wasn't making mistakes—I just wasn't living abundantly. Because my mind never really rested during those five years, my work became meaningless to me. What a tragedy. My FOMO—the root of my hard-driving work ethic—had trumped my joy for my work and my accomplishments.

Is your FOMO robbing you? Consider these statements to be true or false:

- I know God has my career and life mapped out perfectly; I just need to seek his guidance and give each day my all as I pray and obey.
- I never dwell on what might be, should be, or can be; I am content with what *is* this very day.
- Every morning I choose freedom in God's promises over the fear of missing out.

THEIR DAYS OF LABOR ARE FILLED WITH PAIN AND GRIEF; EVEN AT NIGHT THEIR MINDS CANNOT REST. IT IS ALL MEANINGLESS.
ECCLESIASTES 2:23

After I left that position, I planned to work part-time by starting my own consulting firm. My goal was to slow down, enjoy life, and have more time with my family. But within three weeks, my practice was booked for the year with the largest companies in the technology industry. God affirmed my work and blessed my business by showing me that I can choose to overcome a mind-set of fear. So I decided to choose freedom over FOMO. And I get up every morning and choose it again.

DAY 32

A BLOODY KNEE
AT THE FINISH LINE

The only person you are destined to become is the person you decide to be.
RALPH WALDO EMERSON

OUR SON-IN-LAW, ADAM, enjoys running. Our daughter, Shauna, enjoys doing things with Adam—and that's how she found herself filling out a registration form to run a 5K. After weeks of training together, race day finally arrived, and Adam took his place ahead of her in his starting bracket. Standing at the starting line, Shauna was excited, optimistic, prepared, and raring to go. But twenty-five feet into the race, she fell. Hard. Perched on her hands and knees in the middle of the street, she sat dazed, trying to reorient herself as other runners sped past in the frenzy of the crowded start. But then she felt herself rising. Two men lifted her to her feet and said, "Keep going!" Shocked from the fall, with her pants ripped and a knee bloodied, Shauna had a decision to make in a matter of seconds: She could call it a day and say she tried, or she could finish the race.

As she continued on, the crowds, recognizing she was injured, encouraged her and cheered her on: "Don't stop!" "You can do it!" "Keep going!" And in spite of her pain, she did. She kept going. With every step, Shauna made the conscious decision to put one foot in front of the other and persevere through her discomfort and disappointment. Crossing the finish line, bleeding and sore, she realized she only needed two things that day to finish the race: encouragement and determination. She would not give in to the mind game of defeat, and neither would those cheering her on.

To live the abundant life, we must sign up for the race. We must commit to showing up and prepare ourselves for the mind games that are headed our way. As we would gird ourselves for a race, we must invest the time to mentally and physically prepare, day after day. For just a spark of dedication, Christ rewards us with the spiritual stamina we need to make it across the finish line, even after we've stumbled and fallen.

Some of us find ourselves today like Shauna, having suffered disappointments or setbacks. And some of us are like the two men who lifted her; we've been called to support our fellow sister when she's down and out. Others of us are cheering, via our prayers, for those who struggle because we're all in this race together. When we inspire and encourage, we bring out the best in others. When we persevere through our pain, we bear witness to the crowds to our unwavering faith.

So, my friend, a few questions for you to ponder today:

o Have you decided to sign up for this exhilarating race?
o If so, do you daily recommit your life to God?
o Are you well prepared for the mind game you might face when you fail?
o Are you cheering on those in your life who need your support? If not, can you think of someone you can emotionally lift up?

SINCE WE ARE SURROUNDED BY SUCH A HUGE CROWD OF WITNESSES TO THE LIFE OF FAITH, LET US STRIP OFF EVERY WEIGHT THAT SLOWS US DOWN, ESPECIALLY THE SIN THAT SO EASILY TRIPS US UP. AND LET US RUN WITH ENDURANCE THE RACE GOD HAS SET BEFORE US.
HEBREWS 12:1

Years back, one of my New Year's resolutions was to no longer allow a spirit of scarcity to rule my life. Since then I have found I get a second wind by simply calling on Jesus. I can also confidently share with you that the only race I've signed up for and am willing to run is the one for Christ. Jogging is just not my thing.

DAY 33

DIAGNOSIS: PLEASEANOSIS

If you live for people's acceptance, you'll die from their rejection.

LECRAE

IN MY MIND, I AM A TALL WOMAN. I regularly reach for things that are far beyond my grasp. I may stand at five foot four, but I've always thought of myself as much taller. I have often waved off sales associates with a giggle when they insist on bringing me an extra-small blouse. "Oh, I know this will never fit," I say. I truly believe my shoulders are too broad and my arms too long. Steve is most aware of my lack of reality in this regard and finds it amusing. He is my voice of reason, pointing out ever so sweetly that I'm not as tall as I think I am.

I have a disconnect with reality, as I think we all do to some degree. Whether it be our height, our weight, our motivations, our aptitudes, our prejudices, or our temperaments—we all fail, from time to time, to see things as they really are. Sometimes a friend or family member can help us discern fact from fiction, but often we just have to figure it out for ourselves.

And this often comes into play for many women, like myself, who suffer from Pleaseanosis. Desperate to please and not wanting to let others down, we find we can't say "no" to save our lives. Often an acute condition, it can advance to a chronic state when we don't assess the drivers and motivations behind our inability to say no to requests that will spread us too thin. But knowing if we seek to please others in order to satisfy something lacking in our own spirits, or if we're serving specifically for the glory of God, is a good place to start. So take a quiz with me to see where you stand and if you can identify the cause behind the condition. Here we go!

- In the projects or programs you volunteer for or get elected to, do you find yourself complaining incessantly about the people or process?
- Do you get a "feel good" feeling when someone asks you to participate in a project even though you'd rather not?
- Are you more likely to agree to volunteer for a position that you might not otherwise if someone you really admire asks you?
- Does your mind often say no to requests, but your mouth still says yes?
- When you agree to do something you don't want to do or haven't the time to invest in, are you looking to gain someone's respect, approval, or acceptance?

If you answered yes . . .

- One to two times: Good news! You have only a mild case of Pleaseanosis, but beware—this condition can go from mild to severe without much warning. Stay alert and say yes to only those opportunities you feel God is calling you to.
- Three times: Your Pleaseanosis has advanced. Consider declining the next request or invitation unless you have prayed about it and know it is a place of service that will glorify God (and not yourself).
- Four to five times: Your Pleaseanosis has reached a critical stage, but there's good news—it's not terminal. *Just say no.*

MAY THE LORD OUR GOD SHOW US HIS APPROVAL AND MAKE OUR EFFORTS SUCCESSFUL. YES, MAKE OUR EFFORTS SUCCESSFUL!

PSALM 90:17

Saying yes only to the things that glorify God and lift your spirit will keep you from feeling spread thin. They will show you that your worth is far more in God's eyes than in those of any person. Facing this condition, or any that you might struggle with, is an important first step in correcting it. But dealing with reality is hard for me, too. The truth is I'm not even five foot four anymore.

DAY 34

JUDGING OUR JUDGMENT

Too often, we judge other groups by their worst examples
while judging ourselves by our best intentions.

GEORGE W. BUSH
at Dallas Police Memorial, July 12, 2016

WHILE DALLAS WAS mourning the July 7, 2016, shooting of twelve police officers, resulting in five lives lost, there was some deep soul-searching going on all over the city. A rich dialogue between communities, interfaith prayer meetings, and shared grief over inexplicable loss and the realities of racism consumed our thoughts and conversations for weeks following the tragic event. President George W. Bush spoke at the televised memorial for the fallen officers, and his statement convicted me to my core: "Too often, we judge other groups by their worst examples while judging ourselves by our best intentions." How often do we do this? How often do we look at the speck in another's eye without seeing the log in our own?[10]

Everyone seems to have their version of "the truth," when in reality what we hold as fact is only an opinion or stereotype that ultimately has no value or contribution toward a fruitful life. It's a mind game: Just because we think something is so, doesn't make it so. Instead we must look to God and his Word for truth and know it is never our job to judge others.

I think this summing up of others is epidemic in our society, and the public platform that is provided so seamlessly by social media has only caused this virus to spread. I'm absolutely sure it detracts from abundant living for both those being judged and the accusers. Consider these questions to see where you stand:

- Have you made a silent judgment about someone's appearance in the past seventy-two hours but brushed it off as normal?
- Do you find yourself judging other groups of people (millennials, Gen X, baby boomers, Democrats, Republicans, a specific profession, a specific race, etc.) by the poor behavior of a few?
- Have you modeled this behavior by making a judgmental or condescending remark about someone in the past seventy-two hours to your spouse, child, or close friend?
- When you recognize a flaw in others, do you feel a teeny-weeny bit better about yourself?
- Do you think you have become so habitually critical of others that you don't even recognize when you're doing it?

If you answered yes . . .

- One to two times: Even a little bit of judgment is bad—for both your soul and the recipient's heart. Pray that God will reveal to you—in the moment—when you're judging others.
- Three times: Consider what's driving your need to judge. Pray for conviction that God will set your heart right.
- Four to five times: Your judgment could be spreading others and yourself much too thin. Remember that God has created each person in his image. Ask that God will help you to view others through his eyes.

DO NOT JUDGE OTHERS, AND YOU WILL NOT BE JUDGED.
MATTHEW 7:1

Pray with me that God will convict us each and every time we consciously or subconsciously judge or critically condemn others. Pray for help and self-discipline that we will not poison others with this condemnation of our brothers and sisters. To win at this mind game, we often have to be on our toes. Judging and being judged spreads us all too thin.

DAY 35

GRADING YOUR SAT

What we are is God's gift to us. What we become is our gift to God.
ELEANOR POWELL

OUR COMPANY SUBSCRIBES to the *Now, Discover Your Strengths* philosophy developed by Marcus Buckingham and Donald Clifton. The StrengthsFinder assessment that accompanies this philosophy was developed as the result of a Gallup study, which looked at more than two million people who had successful careers. Ultimately this assessment provides individuals with a list of the top five strengths that they naturally possess and explains how each strength can be used to their benefit, both personally and professionally. At my company, we not only require all potential employees to take the assessment, we chart each team member's gifts by department. It's important to us that candidates know how they are hardwired and that we're aware so we can align their gifts with the expectations of the role. It's our collective job to be good stewards of our employees' talents and to use them wisely.

Knowing and embracing your SAT—strengths, aptitude, and talents—as well as your shortcomings, and communicating them well to managers and peers, can fuel the abundant life at work. I've seen this exercised incredibly well for more than twenty years; the success and overall job satisfaction that come when individuals and managers understand and align projects by strengths are very rewarding.

Here's the meat of this philosophy: It is biblical. Our work and how we use the talents God has given us matter greatly to him. The roles he gives us are not just jobs we're filling. Our work is a *calling*, whether we are retail clerks, accountants, teachers, homemakers, engineers, account executives, or in ministry. The job title doesn't matter to God. The excellence with which we use our talents does.

To assess if you're a good steward of your gifts, answer these questions:

- Can you name your top five strengths in the next sixty seconds?
- Are you using your best talents or gifts 80 percent of the week?
- Are you in a role for which you are uniquely or appropriately qualified?
- Do you find yourself energized by your productivity or what you've accomplished at the end of the day?
- Would you choose this role or job over any other? If not, what would you choose?

If you answered no . . .

- One to two times: Awesome! I bet you love what you do—at least most of the time. After all, work is toil. But it should be good toil.
- Three times: Don't give up! If you don't know your top five strengths, search them out. And then pray about how you should put them to work.
- Four to five times: It could be time for a serious reevaluation. Your talents are a God-given gift. Accept the blessing, and then put those talents to good use.

TO THOSE WHO USE WELL WHAT THEY ARE GIVEN, EVEN MORE WILL BE GIVEN, AND THEY WILL HAVE AN ABUNDANCE. BUT FROM THOSE WHO DO NOTHING, EVEN WHAT LITTLE THEY HAVE WILL BE TAKEN AWAY.
MATTHEW 25:29

I love this Scripture. If we use well what we've been given, we will be given more in *abundance*. Sister, we have to know our gifts and talents to take advantage of them.

DAY 36

SIZING YOUR FUSSY PANTS

A keen sense of humor helps us to overlook the unbecoming,
understand the unconventional, tolerate the unpleasant,
overcome the unexpected, and outlast the unbearable.

BILLY GRAHAM

OFTEN WE HAVE THE aptitude for a particular calling but lack the temperament. I think back (a long way back) to my second-grade schoolteacher. She had the appropriate degrees, a full grasp of the curriculum, and more than thirty-five years of teaching experience. But she also had anger management issues. How in the world this woman kept her job year to year in our little country school, I have no idea.

It's telling when a child can see the effect of one's temperament on the greater outcome of an endeavor, and I saw it so clearly, even to the point of sharing it with my parents. Some of us students learned from her, but we never *loved* to learn from her. What a tragedy. Her temperament—not well aligned with her profession—caused many of my classmates to stall out that year. They were so paralyzed with fear that they failed to thrive.

Not everyone is suited for a particular profession or a particular role within that profession. I have made the mistake of promoting someone into a management position for which they possessed all of the aptitude but none of the attitude required to succeed. Neither they nor I was aware of the soft skills they lacked to encourage, develop, mentor, and motivate a team.

A failure to understand just how big our fussy pants really are can spread us too thin. When we're in a position for which our temperament is not well suited, we can find ourselves complaining often and alienating, discouraging, or even hurting others—thereby not only depleting our own enjoyment of a gratifying life but negatively affecting and infecting those around us.

There's a common thread among those whose temperaments are not well aligned with their positions. Let's see if it sounds familiar:

- Are you often out of sorts at the place where you work or volunteer?
- Do you consistently complain about a person, place, or thing that you feel affects your ability to do your job well?
- Do you let a negative attitude at work carry over to other parts of your life?
- Do others avoid objective conversations with you for fear they will ruffle your feathers?
- At the end of the day, would you say you are more emotionally exhausted than physically or mentally spent?

If you answered yes . . .

- One to two times: Good for you. If you're not complaining or someone is not complaining about you, your temperament is probably well suited for your role.
- Three times: Your temperament may be contributing to your feeling spread thin.
- Four to five times: Something's not quite right. Consider if you're "temperamentally hardwired" for what you're doing.

GOD IS WORKING IN YOU, GIVING YOU THE DESIRE AND THE POWER TO DO WHAT PLEASES HIM. DO EVERYTHING WITHOUT COMPLAINING AND ARGUING, SO THAT NO ONE CAN CRITICIZE YOU.

PHILIPPIANS 2:13-15

To opt in to lasting peace, our temperaments must be well suited for our work and workplace. Fussy pants, of *any* size, will always pinch and bind.

DAY 37

THE JOY METER

You have as much laughter as you have faith.

MARTIN LUTHER

WE ALL HAVE A JOY METER—an internal reader of sorts that indicates the degree to which we allow others or difficult circumstances to affect our spiritual, physical, and emotional well-being. We are all affected by the attitudes and actions of others, along with circumstances outside our control; the question is, do we let these things and people impact our joy?

This is a mind game we all need to learn how to win.

Some of us hate to be out of control. We feel our joy meter plummeting when others fail to follow the rules or don't meet our expectations. A work situation that's gone haywire, a family member who is making poor decisions, or a last-minute canceled flight can send some of us off the deep end. We want justice for these situations, for things to be made right in our lives and world—but they don't always happen the way we'd like.

An airline can't make it right when you've missed a full eight hours of your vacation. Judges and juries cannot always discern the truth because of legal loopholes and restrictions. Mothers may try to raise God-honoring children, but those kids don't always turn out as hoped because of free will. Each of these situations and many more leave us wanting because justice is not of our world. It's of the heavens.

Those who have a long history of walking closely with Christ through substantial challenges, disappointments, and loss often find their joy meters working extremely well, even in times of duress. These saints live their lives exemplifying what I call the spiritual three Rs: redemption, reparation, and reliance. They trust God will redeem every bad situation for good. They know he will make right what is wrong. Their reliance on him empowers them to transfer control, allowing their joy meters to operate as they are intended to.

Without understanding what our role is versus God's role when it comes to control, we may struggle to lay claim to our inheritance of an abundant life. On a scale of one to three, with one representing *not at all*; two, *occasionally*; and three, *I'm rocking this*, please rate the following:

- I am able to separate my circumstances from my inner sense of joy and well-being.
- I release anyone and everyone from any sense of obligation that might affect my state of joy, positively or negatively.
- I am able to refrain from allowing my children's failures or unhappiness to affect my joy in the Lord.
- I trust God's hand and promise even in times of challenge or despair.
- Friends and family seek me out as an encourager and light because I have demonstrated joy during a trial or crisis.

Your joy meter reading:

- A score of five to nine might indicate that your need for control allows others to negatively affect the joy that Christ has promised you.
- A score of ten to fourteen could reflect a need to pray for the spiritual three Rs.
- A score of fifteen indicates your joy meter is humming!

You will show me the way of life, granting me the joy of your presence and the pleasures of living with you forever.

PSALM 16:11

No one can mess with your joy—that is, if you're in possession of the three Rs.

DAY 38

A DIGITAL DILEMMA

Clarity about what matters provides clarity about what does not.

CAL NEWPORT, *Deep Work: Rules for Focused Success in a Distracted World*

MY COMPANY MARKETS technology and has done so since 1994. The advancements in this industry not only make for an exciting work experience but provide for my personal daily wants and needs. I tell you this so you can fully understand my position when it comes to digital devices: Technology is one of the best things that our society has experienced, but it is also one of the worst.

Today we get our directions from our phones or the GPS systems in our cars (but mine has gotten me lost). We can talk to anyone anywhere in the world at any time (if we choose to pay the international roaming charges). And we can know what our sister is having for dinner. (But, really, do we care?) I digress. You probably know where this is going. That little phone in our handbag, that computer on our desk, and that tablet in our living room can easily contribute to frantic living. We're connected 24-7, and sister, this isn't biblical.

A few months ago I gave this challenge to our executive staff: *Take a break from e-mail for a couple of hours every day (yes, while at the office). Do not access your e-mail after 6:00 p.m. While standing in line at the checkout counter, don't look at your phone. Pry whatever digital device your children are using out of their chubby little hands. Then tell me about the great, creative ideas you had while your mind was free or the experience you shared with your kids.* Well, you'd think I had sentenced them to Siberia! What? No e-mail for hours? Not at night? Take the tablet from my preschoolers? The kids will go nuts. Yes, they might—and you might—for a short time. It's called withdrawal.

Addiction to anything (even social media via digital devices) spreads us too thin because it replaces our dependency on God with a dependency on an impostor. That dopamine hit that makes us feel validated and accepted, that allows us to escape reality while being entertained, and that gives us the illusion of being "in control" is a lousy substitute for intimacy with our Almighty. We know this addiction has gone too far when nomophobia—the fear of being separated from one's phone—is now a diagnosable disorder. Satan has played a mind game with us, taking something that is very good (technology) and using it as a way to bankrupt our abundant life. After all, how often do you feel depleted, jealous, or angry after spending hours on social media? Don't you wish you had those hours back?

This is not likely to be an easy quiz today. I wish you the best of luck:

- Have you turned your smartphone off or unplugged from your computer in the past forty-eight hours?
- Do you often forget to check Facebook or Instagram?
- Do you typically unplug from e-mail or social networking by 7:00 p.m.?
- Do you have a "no phone at the table" policy when dining with friends or family?
- Have you implemented a "technology-free" weekend for yourself or your family?

If you answered yes . . .

- Four to five times: Good job! You're using technology—it's not using you!
- Two to three times: You're doing okay, but I think you can do better. Make one of these a goal to improve this week.

- One to two times: You are in need of what the author Cal Newport calls an "Internet Sabbath." NOW.

DON'T BE DEJECTED AND SAD, FOR THE JOY OF THE LORD IS YOUR STRENGTH!
NEHEMIAH 8:10

I know it's hard to unplug and even harder to listen to the kids whine and complain. But don't become a slave to technology. Instead, invest your time in your family and the talents God's given you. That lasting peace you're looking for is found in him.

DAY 39

THE THREE FS OF CRAY CRAY:
FRIENDS, FOES, AND FAMILY

*It's not that I don't like people. It's just that when I'm
in the company of others—even my nearest and dearest—
there always comes a moment when I'd rather be reading a book.*
MAUREEN CORRIGAN, *Leave Me Alone, I'm Reading:
Finding and Losing Myself in Books*

PEOPLE, MORE OFTEN than circumstances, can be short-term drainers
to our sense of well-being. There are three primary drivers that affect
me personally: First, Satan will do anything and everything to come
between me and every godly relationship I have. Second, because I am
a relater (defined as someone who derives a great deal of pleasure and
energy from their close relationships—both personal and professional),
I am naturally invested deeply in those I care for. Third, I let them.

I have learned that our peeps can completely unravel our joy—*if* we
allow them to. For those of us who are married and/or have children,
it's often hard to distinguish where we begin and they end. My identity
is as tightly woven to Steve, Scott, Shauna, Adam, and Ava as the finest
Rwandan basket. But I can also list another thirty people with whom
I share a close friendship or shared vision and reciprocal dependency.
These are also my peeps. And they, too, can make me nuts!

You also may struggle with the degree to which you allow those
closest to you to derail your joy. But the answer should be "to no
degree." This includes those in your life who may have betrayed you,
abandoned you, or caused you great pain. No one has a right to impede
on or affect what is the result of your salvation through Christ. God

gave up his Son for you so that you might have the promise of abundant life. Remember that incredible, undeserved gift the next time you're tempted to say, "I'd have a lot more joy if . . ."

Let's assess if our friends, foes, and family might be affecting our state of lasting peace:

- Do you carefully invest in your own self-care and spiritual development before sacrificing your well-being for others?
- Are you consistent at speaking the truth in love when it's appropriate and called for?
- Do you demonstrate honest, open communication rather than a passive-aggressive spirit?
- With those in your life who might be hurtful or even caustic, can you love them while keeping your boundaries intact?
- Do you forgive and forget a past wrongdoing rather than allowing it to play over and over in your head?

If you answered yes . . .

- Four to five times: Good job! Your joy is clearly seated in your salvation!
- Two to three times: Now that you know you're not living the abundant life promised by your salvation, how can you work to restore your joy and thus bring joy to others as well?
- One to two times: Consider what role you will allow others to play in your life and seek God through prayer in claiming his wonderful inheritance that brings abundant joy.

MAY THE GOD OF HOPE FILL YOU WITH ALL JOY AND PEACE IN BELIEVING, SO THAT BY THE POWER OF THE HOLY SPIRIT YOU MAY ABOUND IN HOPE.
ROMANS 15:13, ESV

I love all my peeps. I love them dearly. But they can't have my joy because I love Jesus more.

DAY 40

THE SHAME GAME

Shame is a soul eating emotion.
CARL JUNG

ONE OF THE MOST IMPORTANT mind games we must assess has nothing to do with people or places or things. It has to do with the soul-eating condition inside our hearts and minds when we fail to move past our shame.

Shame, in its proper context, is not all bad. Considered one of the deepest and even most paralyzing of feelings, it has its place. The embarrassment we feel as the result of doing something wrong was designed by God to convict us of our mistakes in order to draw us back to him. Shame, depending on how it's managed and dealt with, can either play a vital role in our state of lasting peace—providing us new life via forgiveness and repentance—or feed us a steady diet of despair, driving us to a place that will keep us ever separated from the relationship and life Christ longs to share with us.

I know shame. I know what it looks like and how it acts. Even among God-honoring women, I have witnessed the dreadful decisions friends and family have made to cloak their shame in order to shield themselves from the consequences of their mistakes. More often than not, the result of the cover-up turns out to be much worse than the original error. Shame knows how to play all types of mind games with us, starting with the one that lies and says, "There's no way out of this but to . . ." It tempts us to doubt God's forgiveness of our sins—a forgiveness that is absolute. But that's shame. Two can play at this game, and we have the Master on our side of the board. But to boot shame out of the tournament once and for all, *we have to tag him in.*

There's no quiz today, just a few questions for you to consider before you sit down to visit with your Redeemer.

- Do you know that God knew about your sin before you were even born and loves you so much that he sent his Son to die on a cross for that very sin?
- Do you know that he loves you unconditionally; there's nothing you have done or will do that will cause him to love you more or love you less?
- Do you know he rose from the grave *specifically* so you could live with him for eternity, in spite of that sin?
- Do you know there's nothing you need to do to receive that gift but to ask him to forgive you?
- Can you ask him for his forgiveness for that sin—one last time? And this time, will you accept it?

THOSE WHO LOOK TO HIM FOR HELP WILL BE RADIANT WITH JOY;
NO SHADOW OF SHAME WILL DARKEN THEIR FACES.

PSALM 34:5

O Lord, hear my cry for my sweet sister. Father, guide her to release this shame so she can come alive and be made new. May she live the profoundly rich life you've given her through your Son's sacrifice. Let her joy be complete. In the name of your Son, Christ Jesus, I pray. Amen.

DAY 41

COMING UP SHORT

Know, first, who you are; and then adorn yourself accordingly.

EPICTETUS

WOMEN HAVE LIKELY compared themselves to others ever since Eve's first daughter could gaze up at her mother. As young girls, many of us looked to our mommies to help us project our future. As we grew, we compared ourselves in size, shape, beauty, intellect, personality, and character. I thought for sure I was destined to be a five-foot-eight-inch blonde bombshell. (I am not.) It seems to be in our nature to compare. As we take these side-by-side evaluations with us into our teens and adulthood, the sport of comparison is taken to the next level as we measure ourselves against our sisters and our peers.

It's no secret that I am not a fan of Facebook or Instagram. I agree that there is substantial benefit in using social media to communicate viable information quickly to the masses, but a journal of what one tried on in the dressing room last Saturday is not something I see as a personal or societal benefit. What concerns me more than the time sink these sites have become are the feelings of inadequacy, lost opportunity, shorted blessings, and loneliness they have fed so easily to so many, spreading them way too thin. The craziest thing about it all is that the cat is already out of the bag: Even though everyone *knows* that no one's life is as perfect as it might appear online, people still compare their lives to others', bankrupting themselves of their joy and discounting their blessings!

This sport of comparison is like trying to pole-vault over a bar we can't clear because someone else raises the bar higher just as we approach. We try harder, we strategize, we reach, but we continue to fall short. The maddest part of this scenario is that we know the bar is an illusion—it's not even real, but we keep running at it, jumping toward it anyway, feeling like a failure when we miss.

Unlike any other moment in time, our society has become one of posture. What we look like to others has begun to take precedence over who we really are, and that should trigger some alarm bells for our Christian community. Sister, you are really, really important as you are and especially for *who* you are. You are not portraying a made-up image. You are the real deal.

I am definitely the odd man out among my contemporaries concerning this position, but humor me. In the context of opting out of frantic living,

- Would you have more or less joy if you spent fewer hours watching what everyone else was doing and started doing something meaningful yourself?
- Have you compared yourself to others, via their posts, and felt you were somehow shortchanged or short-blessed?
- Do you know most people only post their happiest times or even their own illusion of their happiest moments online?
- Knowing this, do you feel inadequate anyway?

OH YES, YOU SHAPED ME FIRST INSIDE, THEN OUT; YOU FORMED ME IN MY MOTHER'S WOMB. I THANK YOU, HIGH GOD—YOU'RE BREATHTAKING! BODY AND SOUL, I AM MARVELOUSLY MADE!
PSALM 139:13-14, MSG

No matter what you see on social media, know it's not reality. Their marriage is not perfect (I bet you a roll of Charmin he leaves the toilet seat up). Their kids are not perfect either; they're teenagers! Their degrees, pedigrees, and 100K "likes" don't change who they are. And it doesn't change who you are, either. Ignore the bar. It's an illusion Satan has created to take your eye off the real goal: to live abundantly with Christ.

DAY 42

FRAIDY CAT

Don't lose yourself on the way to the top.

JACK WELCH

IT WAS THE FOURTH OF JULY and hot as hades that evening in Texas when Steve and I decided not to fight the crowds to watch the fireworks. We lived on a lake and knew the fireworks were set off from a barge, so we decided to shimmy up to the roof of our covered patio and take in the show with our kids, who were about ten and thirteen at the time.

As dusk settled in, we scouted out our path up the railing to the roof of the house and over to the roof of the patio. *Easy peasy.* We enjoyed a fabulous fireworks display with absolutely no traffic jam— that is, until it was time for me to climb down. I soon came to find out I was really good at shimmying up but a total fraidy cat at climbing down. Who knew? The kids laughed hysterically at my sudden "freeze," as Steve lovingly encouraged and coaxed me (as one would a child) inch by inch off the roof under a pitch-black sky. For this reason, I have not gone—nor ever will go—rock climbing. I'm pretty sure I could go up, but I definitely know I couldn't get down.

Climbing up the corporate ladder during the early years of my career was quite similar. I had no trouble scaling up the enterprise, but my trouble came when I couldn't see clearly how to remove myself from my ninth-floor perch. I knew in my heart that my career—something I enjoyed greatly—was in conflict with my desire for abundant living. I even knew it was fueling scarcity in the form of physical, emotional, and mental tolls, but for the life of me, I wasn't sure how I was going to give it up. Then, one Sunday morning during this period of conflict (also known as conviction), a new sermon series was introduced at church, and the topic that morning was about our treasure—"For where your treasure is, there will your heart be also" (Matthew 6:21, KJV). Well, of course it was! Convicting sermons preached by godly men always seem to surface when they need to.

The Holy Spirit whispered (actually it was more like an announcement through a bullhorn) that my work, my position, my career had become my treasure. I realized in less than thirty minutes that I was forfeiting an uncommon life because I was fearful of coming down from what was familiar, from what I had given so much of my life to. I felt uneasy regarding the impact my departure would make on my company and team, unsure about what I'd do to fill my days, unclear as to how I would replace my salary, and uncertain that I even knew who I was beyond my role as vice president of merchandising. I got up that ladder with no problem. Coming down was tricky.

Identifying if your position in your company or community has come between you and an abundant life is important. Are you in a position at work or in your volunteer organization that . . .

- You know is affecting your ability to live a satisfying life to the fullest?
- Is dictated more by economics or responsibility to others than God's calling?
- In your heart you know its season has ended—but you're not sure how to come down?

I HOLD YOU BY YOUR RIGHT HAND—I, THE LORD YOUR GOD.
AND I SAY TO YOU, "DON'T BE AFRAID. I AM HERE TO HELP YOU."
ISAIAH 41:13

What had been so hard for me to sort through for months became crystal clear in half an hour. God has a way of guiding us down and planting our feet on solid ground. Just listen for the cues.

DAY 43

GETTING IT OVER THE NET

Dear friends, never take revenge. Leave that to the righteous anger of God.
For the Scriptures say, "I will take revenge; I will pay them back," says the LORD.
ROMANS 12:19

TENNIS IS NOT A GAME I have ever mastered. I can serve pretty well, but getting that little yellow booger of a ball over the net consistently takes a great deal of coordination, effort, and expertise that I do not have. After an hour or so of playing the game, I can safely say I feel drained and defeated—and I'm sure I look silly while playing.

There is another game that we can unwittingly get caught up in that leaves us exhausted: It's the sport of tit for tat, or the volley of retribution and paybacks. A word that cuts deeply or a slight that threatens one's self-esteem is usually the serve that drives the return. Unlike a tennis match, this game can go on forever with no winners, just losers—including those watching from the sidelines.

I have watched these games play out over the years and have found that it is rarely the seriousness of the offense itself that gets the game going. I've even seen the volley begin when the offense was made unintentionally! But once it starts, a spirit of justice begins to stir in the players. In business, this game can get ugly and go into extra sets depending on the pride or ego of the individuals. In families, it can lead to division and separation. The bitterness and unforgiving spirits that result become heavy weights we lug around, and, sister, they are not conducive to living the abundant life. Retaliation—even just thinking about it—will spread any of us too thin. Peace and paybacks cannot coexist in that same pretty little head.

Some questions to consider:

- Do you spend any portion of any day thinking about someone who has intentionally or even unintentionally wronged you?
- Have you thought of ways you would pay them back or hurt them emotionally for this wrong?
- Does this mode of thinking bring you joy and peace or anger and bitterness?
- Have you considered how much better you'd feel if you just forgave them?
- What blessing do you think might await you if you were to actually empathize *with* this person and their grievances?

ALL OF YOU SHOULD BE OF ONE MIND. SYMPATHIZE WITH EACH OTHER. LOVE EACH OTHER AS BROTHERS AND SISTERS. BE TENDERHEARTED, AND KEEP A HUMBLE ATTITUDE. DON'T REPAY EVIL FOR EVIL. DON'T RETALIATE WITH INSULTS WHEN PEOPLE INSULT YOU. INSTEAD, PAY THEM BACK WITH A BLESSING. THAT IS WHAT GOD HAS CALLED YOU TO DO, AND HE WILL GRANT YOU HIS BLESSING. FOR THE SCRIPTURES SAY, "IF YOU WANT TO ENJOY LIFE AND SEE MANY HAPPY DAYS, KEEP YOUR TONGUE FROM SPEAKING EVIL AND YOUR LIPS FROM TELLING LIES. TURN AWAY FROM EVIL AND DO GOOD. SEARCH FOR PEACE, AND WORK TO MAINTAIN IT."

1 PETER 3:8-11

One of the most famous quotes of all time on this topic, attributed to Gandhi, is "An eye for an eye makes the whole world blind." But I like Jesus' words even better: "This is my command: Love each other" (John 15:17).

DAY 44

THINK OF THEM AS A
FOREIGN MISSION FIELD

Be kind, for everyone you meet is fighting a hard battle.
ATTRIBUTED TO IAN MACLAREN

WE ALL SERVE SOMEONE. If you work in the health industry, you care for patients. If you're in ministry, you "tend" your sheep. If you are a volunteer, teacher, or cashier, or if you're employed by a service organization such as ours, you serve students, customers, or clients. And it's likely that from time to time they will *wear you out*. Yes, ma'am. No one can spread you thinner than a difficult customer.

Serving others is really fun when they're being patient, kind, and appreciative. Serving them when they're on their last nerve is a different story. This is when a spirit of ministry needs to kick in. I have found when I am faced with an unreasonable demand or unhappy customer, I need to think of that person as a mission field: He or she is desperate for relief.

At our agency, our first core value—the tenet by which we operate—is *service*. To us, serving is not an obligation or something we have to do to set ourselves apart from other agencies. Service is a privilege. God has blessed us with unique gifts, opportunities, and fabulous clients, and it is our responsibility to be good stewards of those talents, protecting ourselves from burnout when difficult circumstances or challenging individuals begin to affect our attitude and quality of service.

Being burned out by our jobs will dilute us quicker than anything else—after all, we spend forty-plus hours of our week there. Becoming overextended and exasperated by another's demands often leads to disappointment and a feeling of defeat or failure. The fallout not only affects us personally, but it can threaten the state of peace and security in our families, depending on what we choose to take home. To prevent this, we must guard our minds and center our hearts to respond with grace the next time we face a challenging person. We must pray for strength in order to counter their anger with kindness. We must choose to bring light into their dark world, just as we would the needy and oppressed in faraway lands.

Just between you and me,

○ Are your customers, students, patients, clients, or teammates becoming a frustration to the point of negatively impacting your joy for your work?
○ Can you consider that outside circumstances are likely making their lives difficult too?
○ Would you think differently about how you serve them if you considered them more as your ministry than as customers or peers?

LIVE WISELY AMONG THOSE WHO ARE NOT BELIEVERS, AND MAKE THE MOST OF EVERY OPPORTUNITY. LET YOUR CONVERSATION BE GRACIOUS AND ATTRACTIVE SO THAT YOU WILL HAVE THE RIGHT RESPONSE FOR EVERYONE.
COLOSSIANS 4:5-6

Pray for patience. Put a smile on that pretty face. And play this mind game to win.

DAY 45

THE SKINNY MIRROR

If you could kick the person in the pants responsible
for most of your trouble, you wouldn't sit for a month.
THEODORE ROOSEVELT

I LOVE A GOOD SKINNY MIRROR. I bet you know what I'm talking about—those mirrors that reflect yourself, only about five pounds lighter. They're often found in hotels, and I just love it when I find one in our room. Over the duration of my entire vacation, I look awesome.

The problem, of course, with a good skinny mirror is that you don't see yourself the way you truly are. Clothes that look good in a dressing room don't look quite the same when you try them on at home; suddenly bulges and paunches appear. While on vacation, the illusion cast by a skinny mirror might compel a person to overeat—or at least it did for this one. A self-inflicted scam, I call it. We're easily tricked by our mind's eye to believe we look or behave in ways that we don't.

If we want to live with excellence, we must be alert and willing to see things as they really are—and I'm not referring to our physiques here. We have to assess ourselves in the correct light to get a true reflection of our negativity. Sweet sister, I write this to you with humility and grace because I, too, often suffer from a negative attitude. Others can readily see—and are directly affected by—what I've fooled myself into believing is well disguised.

Negativity seems to be the trait many of us don't see when we look at ourselves. Because it tends to creep into our psyches, we unwittingly sabotage our careers, relationships, and reputations. As I witnessed the implosion of two incredibly talented women whose chronic pessimism destroyed their careers, I was at a loss as to how to help. Even when they were counseled repeatedly by others, they couldn't see their negativity in themselves.

And yet we're just as guilty of this. Rather than being the people we desire to be—people of encouragement and hope—we instead see only the failings of everyone and everything around us. We become instigators of gossip, and we don a judgmental spirit. As we age and allow this illusion to continue, we become disgruntled with the world. Grumpy old men and bitter old women wouldn't act the way they do if they were holding up a true mirror.

But this is not about them; this is about you. When you look into your mirror, ask yourself,

- Am I a person others want to be around?
- Do I attempt to encourage someone every day?
- Do I look for the good or positive in every situation?

If the answer is no, blame that old faulty mirror you've been staring into, and go get yourself a real one—one that reflects who you truly are.

DON'T ACT THOUGHTLESSLY, BUT UNDERSTAND WHAT THE LORD WANTS YOU TO DO.
EPHESIANS 5:17

Negativity is a direct reflection of our state of frantic living, while positivity reflects our state of peace. I'm pulling out a real mirror to assess mine, too.

DAY 46

BEING RIGHT

I'm often wrong, but never in doubt.

IVY BAKER PRIEST

STANDING IN OUR KITCHEN, I asked our then-eight-year-old grand-daughter, Ava, if she'd like some instruction. With a mixing bowl in hand and a plan in place, she shook her head no, ready to begin. When Ava visits for her monthly sleepover, a typical Saturday afternoon includes several rounds of *Chopped Junior*. No, we don't watch the famed cooking show for tweens on the Food Network. *We reenact it.*

I select approximately five to six very random ingredients, and she has thirty minutes to create and prepare the dish with those selected items. Then she chooses a variety of bizarre ingredients for me, and I, in kind, must invent a recipe and prepare it. Once the dish is complete, we sample it—regardless of how delicious or disgusting it is. *This game goes on for hours.* On one particular day, I gave her several ingredients that would require her to think through—or at least inquire of me—the possible reaction or outcome of combining such ingredients and the cooking technique she would use. In her "mystery bag" she found a box of Bisquick, frozen blueberries, vanilla ice cream, a mango Popsicle, and pretzels. She placed the Popsicle in the microwave to be served as a bev-erage and melted the ice cream to mix into the Bisquick. All was going well until she decided that her "scone" would be topped with beautiful (albeit frozen) blueberries, tossed with pretzels. As she placed her dessert in the oven, I offered my counsel again, knowing just how those blue-berries would turn to mush. However, with confidence, she stated she was certain she had all the information she needed. Steve will tell you that this little apple didn't fall far from her grandmother's tree.

"Often wrong, but never in doubt" is a quote I have heard from my dear husband since we were married in 1990. Lovingly, he will point out when my confidence overrides my patience to wait for more information; my humility to ask questions and seek advice; and my resourcefulness to research deeper. Each time is a total drainer, especially when I realize that all I had to do to create a better outcome was to resign myself to the fact that someone else had some of the important answers I needed.

No matter the profession, seasoned workers can fall into this trap. Because of our years of experience of doing things a certain way or a stubborn spirit that refuses to be taught, we stand firm in our own ways. But we'd be wise to remain alert so that we don't wake up one day spread too thin by the intellectual demands of a changing workplace. We must remain open-minded and humble, lest our influence become diminished.

We will lose this mind game when we choose to keep our minds closed, in protection of our pride. How well are you playing the game?

- Do you often believe you have all the answers?
- Do you allow your confidence to trump your patience, humility, or resourcefulness?
- Can you recall a situation where, if you'd only asked for help, your outcome would have been different?

MY CHILD, LISTEN TO WHAT I SAY, AND TREASURE MY COMMANDS.
TUNE YOUR EARS TO WISDOM, AND CONCENTRATE ON UNDERSTANDING.
CRY OUT FOR INSIGHT, AND ASK FOR UNDERSTANDING.

PROVERBS 2:1-3

It didn't take long for Ava to realize her mistake. For a child, she's become quite the chef in the kitchen and mastered more than the art of cooking; she's mastered the art of seeking advice. We'd be wise to do the same.

DAY 47

WHAT'S ON YOUR MIND?

CONNECTED BY A SUPERHIGHWAY, our thoughts and feelings race back and forth from our hearts to our minds. Is what we think honoring and gracious? Is what we feel humbling and uplifting? Satan is often cruising this thoroughfare, trying as he might to direct us off course; thus what we think or convince ourselves of is not always trustworthy. Our judgments and presumptions can imprison us to falsehood. Our resentment can sabotage a life of lasting peace. And our fear of missing out can separate us from our inheritance of an abundant life. There is no doubt that we play mind games with ourselves—and with Satan—on a daily basis. And there's no doubt *we can win*.

In Romans 8:5-6 the apostle Paul understood these mind games when he wrote, "Those who live according to the flesh have their minds set on what the flesh desires; but those who live in accordance with the Spirit have their minds set on what the Spirit desires. The mind governed by the flesh is death, but the mind governed by the Spirit is life and peace."[11] The promise of a prosperous, meaningful life will never be realized by feelings and thoughts that are fixed on this world and our own selfish desires. Instead the truth and righteousness of God will lead us there.

Just as we desire to do better and be better, we must commit to thinking better. Knowing you can win these mind games, please prayerfully consider these questions:

- Do you invite God into your thoughts?
- What does he see there?
- Will you pray for guidance and power to think only those thoughts that glorify him?

TO YOU, O LORD,

We profess your greatness and power. To you, Father, we ascribe all glory and majesty. Because of you, our God, we know we can claim victory over any and every mind game.

We bring our Pleaseanosis to you, confessing that we often seek to please others over you. We ask your forgiveness when we squander precious days of abundance to wallow in resentment. Our recurring sins and moral failures dishonor you, and we pray for your forgiveness as we turn away from these sins in order to serve you better. We commit to replace our shortsighted thinking of scarcity with the promise of an abundant life.

Thank you for our gifts, Father! You have equipped us with every talent and strength we need to do your will. We praise you for our customers, coworkers, and family—even, and especially, when they are difficult! We are excited about embracing an uncommon life of lasting peace. We ask for your divine intervention to help us replace our fear of missing out with contentment, our shame with courage and honor, our fear with determination, and our lack of confidence with a new understanding of our unmistakable identity as daughters of the King. This day and every day, Father God, we pray you replace our desire to be blessed with a passion to be the blessing. Give us victory in every mind game that is played—and to you be the glory.

In the name of your Son, Christ Jesus our Savior, we pray. Amen.

PART 3

STRENGTH TRAINING *for the* LONG RUN

DAY 48

STAMINA

Endurance precedes success.
WAYNE CHIRISA

THERE ARE THOUSANDS OF things in this world that I can't do, and some of these things start at the local gym. For starters, I can't do the splits; I can't do pull-ups (the manly kind); nor can I do that flippy thing at the end of the pool when I'm swimming laps. These are just three of the innumerable things that I have failed to master. *Yet.* Just as I know that commitment and endurance are required for me to achieve my goals at the gym, so, too, are they required for me to grasp and hold on to the abundant life. Both take dedication, practice, focus, a change in habit, a change in attitude, and *a really good trainer.*

Transformation of the body begins not in our muscles but in our hearts and minds. However, we don't achieve a particular level of success in a sport simply because we want it. Instead, we must physically work to achieve our goals. And like a physical transformation, a spiritual one requires effort. Christ often stirs something within us, sometimes as the result of a loss or disappointment or sometimes upon hearing his Word, which blesses us and urges us to seek a new way. But just wanting a life of lasting peace will not make it so.

Once something new is learned and adopted—like growing in the Christian faith—fearless determination is required to activate change, especially when it comes to attitudes, habits, and ways of thinking. To shift from a life that has us spread too thin to a life that is rich and fulfilling requires commitment to the practice and strength training for the long run.

Just as I cannot learn new physical skills without dedicated gym time and a good coach, neither can we learn techniques and insight to live a life according to God's purpose without committing to spending time in his Word and calling on the power of the greatest trainer ever—Christ.

When I fail to meet my goals at the gym, it's often because I rely on my own understanding and try to go it alone. When we find ourselves overwhelmed by frantic living, it is often because we've failed to allow Christ and his teachings to be our model and guide. On top of this a gnawing sense of self-defeat can loom over us at the gym (before we even get started!), and I'm afraid that same fear plagues many of us when we think about the changes required to transform our ways to abide with the abundant life. We all love the promise of the outcome, but what it takes to get there is a bit intimidating.

As we consider our strength training for the long run, consider the following questions:

o Does the word *endurance* sound empowering or frightening to you?
o Do you have the information and understanding you need to transform your attitude, habits, and reactions?
o If yes, are you exercising that knowledge, or is it sitting dormant?

MY SPIRIT IS ABIDING IN YOUR MIDST; DO NOT FEAR!
HAGGAI 2:5, NASB

Often it is the fear of the unknown or fear that we're going to have to give up something we enjoy that keeps us from transforming our barren lives to lives of significance. When we think about the awesome power of our Trainer, we should feel strengthened. He's just waiting for us to show up for our session.

DAY 49

COOKING ON ALL FIVE BURNERS

Over the margins of life comes a whisper, a faint call, a premonition of richer living which we know we are passing by. Strained by the very mad pace of our daily outer burdens, we are further strained by an inward uneasiness, because we have hints that there is a way of life vastly richer and deeper than all this hurried existence, a life of unhurried serenity and peace and power.

THOMAS KELLY, *A Testament of Devotion*

MY FIRST KITCHEN upgrade back in the mid-1990s afforded me an extravagance that every cook longs for: a five-burner cooktop. Holy macaroni, I was in Betty Crocker heaven the day it was installed! I purposefully planned a meal that required my firing up all five burners at once. By the time I sat down with the family to eat, my mascara was smeared and my hair was as flat as a corn tortilla from all the steam. Needless to say, I was completely exhausted from stirring, simmering, sautéing, and sweating! My five-burner stove that was so cool one minute was overwhelming an hour later.

During the time of my kitchen remodel, *my life* was like cooking on five burners every minute of every day. Commuting nearly an hour one way to a job that was extremely challenging—while managing a household, raising teenagers, and volunteering at church—I found myself spread so thin from the stress of the responsibility that I began to suffer memory lapses. The concern that I was developing early-onset dementia was the seed to a growing suspicion that this wasn't the abundant life God had promised. Instead this was the "abundant life" of Martha.

If you're not familiar with the New Testament story, Mary and

Martha were sisters who were hosting Jesus at their home. While Mary sat at the feet of Jesus, eager to learn his truth in order to know and love him more deeply, Martha was futzing around the kitchen trying to make everything perfect for the gathering. When she spotted Mary sitting with Jesus, she asked Jesus,

> "LORD, DOESN'T IT SEEM UNFAIR TO YOU THAT MY SISTER JUST SITS HERE WHILE I DO ALL THE WORK? TELL HER TO COME AND HELP ME." BUT THE LORD SAID TO HER, "MY DEAR MARTHA, YOU ARE WORRIED AND UPSET OVER ALL THESE DETAILS! THERE IS ONLY ONE THING WORTH BEING CONCERNED ABOUT. MARY HAS DISCOVERED IT, AND IT WILL NOT BE TAKEN AWAY FROM HER."
>
> LUKE 10:40-42

These wonderful but demanding lives we live can distract us from what really should be our priority. My Viking stove was awesome and fun, but taken to the extreme it proved to be exhausting, leaving me no energy or enthusiasm for the better part of the meal—the fellowship with my family! As modern-day Marthas, we must prevent the good, fun, engaging, demanding, and sometimes even important things that tax us from making us miss what is truly critical.

When it comes to the consideration of your existence, which of these statements do you find true for you?

- I am cooking on all five burners, exhausted and spread thin, but I don't see a need to change anything.
- I know there is a vastly richer way to live, but I have yet to make the changes I need to in order to live it.
- I'm turning off one of my burners to embrace the "better way."

When we built our current house, we installed a five-burner cooktop. Only on the rarest of occasions do I use all five elements at the same time. Now that I have found Mary's better way, I use the Crock-Pot.

DAY 50

PICKING UP THE BATON

The conductor of an orchestra doesn't make a sound.
He depends, for his power, on his ability to make other people powerful.
BENJAMIN ZANDER

I LOVE WATCHING GOOD choir directors or conductors and hearing the fabulous music they are able to draw from their choir or orchestra. Sometimes animated but always focused, they inspire, motivate, and even coax a performance to near perfection. And they do all of this without ever singing a note or picking up an instrument. They are masters in delegation.

For most of my career, I served in positions that required I trust others for a project's overall success, but there were times when I either wanted to do something myself (spurred by pride of achievement), felt I had to do it because others were incapable (caused by a sense of superiority), or lacked the resource pool to effectively delegate (created by my own poor planning). Whatever the reason, I learned one thing: When I try to do everything myself, my work product suffers and frustration sets in.

But it wasn't just in my work that I struggled to delegate. That throbbing in my temples never stayed at the office; it always followed me home. To be the SuperMom I felt I was expected to be, I failed to delegate chores and other responsibilities to my children, especially when they were old enough to contribute. That is, until one day I came across this passage in Exodus, which got my attention:

WHEN MOSES' FATHER-IN-LAW SAW ALL THAT MOSES WAS
DOING FOR THE PEOPLE, HE ASKED, "WHAT ARE YOU REALLY

ACCOMPLISHING HERE? WHY ARE YOU TRYING TO DO ALL THIS
ALONE WHILE EVERYONE STANDS AROUND YOU FROM MORNING
TILL EVENING? . . . THIS IS NOT GOOD! . . . YOU'RE GOING TO
WEAR YOURSELF OUT—AND THE PEOPLE, TOO. THIS JOB IS TOO
HEAVY A BURDEN FOR YOU TO HANDLE ALL BY YOURSELF."

EXODUS 18:14, 17-18

Amazing! Even Moses, God's own chosen servant to lead the
Israelites out of Egypt and bring them to the Promised Land, suffered from the inability to delegate. I love when Moses' father-in-law
tells him, "You're going to wear yourself out—and the people, too."
Yes. This is what happens when we're spread too thin. We convince
ourselves that no one else can solve these complex business issues or
get dinner on the table but us, frustrating ourselves and ultimately
everyone else around us.

Consider your answers to these questions to determine if failing to
delegate might be at the root of your feeling spread thin:

- Would your coworkers or family describe you as a conductor
  or someone who tries to play all the instruments by herself?
- Are you better at delegating at work or home?
- Can you take the skill set that makes you better in one area
  and apply it to the other?

My biggest trouble with delegating was always rooted in trust. But
once I accepted that I could not do everything on my own and learned
that entrusting responsibilities to others grew them and built them up,
I began to let go. Like Benjamin Zander said in today's opening quote,
my direction allowed others to become powerful—and that brought
me peace.

DAY 51

DRIVING WITH
THE TOP DOWN

There cannot be a crisis next week. My schedule is already full.
SECRETARY OF STATE HENRY A. KISSINGER

SEVERAL YEARS AGO, Steve had a convertible sports car. I bought this very cool Katharine Hepburn–like scarf, donned large sunglasses, and put my feet up on the dash (much to Steve's chagrin) as we drove around White Rock Lake with the radio blaring. We always made time for these drives, knowing they provided us breathing room and space from our otherwise busy agendas. And sister, when we live a life with margin, it's like driving with the top down. It's freedom without the tangles.

Margin is having "extra." It's the "white space" in our lives and is important in order to live the abundant life—especially when it comes to our money, time, and forgiveness.

If we're consistently living on the financial edge, we'll miss an important element of the abundant life. There was a time when I lived on a very meager salary; I was a champion coupon clipper, discount shopper, and saver. Yep, on a budget that would make a mouse squeak. But I always made sure to save. Why? Because I needed to have money in the bank in order to give it away. It may sound strange, but this is how it works: If we don't have money available to tithe or give to someone in *greater need than ourselves*, we will live an "all about me" existence. I found the more I could give away, the more peace and joy I gained.

The most precious commodity for many of us is time. I fear our society has forgotten the value of a few unscheduled hours a day. Shoot! Some of us don't even have thirty minutes that are not accounted for! If we have no margin of time, how can we ever be available to minister to our friends and family when they are in need? God may want to use us in extraordinary ways, and yet how often do we miss those opportunities? Imagine if Ananias of Damascus was overscheduled and did not have time to obey God's call to lay hands on Saul and restore his sight (see Acts 9). The conversion of the apostle Paul might never have happened! We have to have a margin of time built into our lives so that we may participate in a miracle, if and when we're called.

We also need to make space in our lives for forgiveness. When we harbor a grudge and withhold forgiveness, we rob ourselves of peace. We think we're punishing the person at fault, but *we're* really the ones getting cheated. We have to practice forgiveness daily so that forgiving becomes easier and easier over time. As long as we live in this fallen world, people, including ourselves, will continue to cause hurt and pain. So we better stock up.

Does driving around in a convertible sound freeing and fun? Wait until you live your life with margin! Do any of these speak to your heart?

- Lord, I need to manage my money better. Direct me with your wisdom, provide me discipline, and bless me with a charitable spirit.
- Lord, I am always running late. I am tired and feel like all I do is go from one thing to the next. Guide me that I might be available for others for when you want to bless me with a *divine appointment.*
- Lord, forgive me that I have not forgiven. Renew my heart, soul, and mind with your love and the forgiveness you've extended to me (over and over and over).

THE MASTER WAS FULL OF PRAISE. "WELL DONE, MY GOOD AND
FAITHFUL SERVANT. YOU HAVE BEEN FAITHFUL IN HANDLING
THIS SMALL AMOUNT, SO NOW I WILL GIVE YOU MANY MORE
RESPONSIBILITIES. LET'S CELEBRATE TOGETHER!"
MATTHEW 25:21

Margin means having extra. Abundance means an oversufficient
supply. But we'll never experience either if we keep running out of the
basic elements.

DAY 52

THE IRONMAN TRIATHLON

Our greatest fear should not be of failure,
but of succeeding at something that doesn't really matter.
D. L. MOODY

ALTHOUGH I HAVE ENJOYED physical activities such as cycling and swimming for the past thirty years, I am not an athlete. I consider exercise as little more than a basic requirement of good stewardship for the earthly body God has blessed me with (and a good counter to an occasional bowl of ice cream). However, Steve and I have enjoyed the company of both men and women who, over the years, have competed in Ironman or half Ironman competitions. The training is grueling. How does one really prepare for a 2.4-mile swim, a 112-mile bike ride (on one of those skinny bicycle seats), and then a 26.2-mile run—a full marathon? Could there be any other requirement? Yes. A full Ironman must be completed in seventeen hours or less. Good grief! I couldn't do this over seventeen months!

For athletes who compete in such extreme events as these, things like sleep, professional advancement, free time with friends and family, and physical comfort come second. These athletes train early in the morning and again after work, they forfeit work or leisure opportunities that compete for their time and attention, and all aches and pains are accepted as part of the process. Clearly there are sacrifices. But this is all done with one huge honkin' goal: to stake their claim as an Ironman. Is the sacrifice worth the blood, sweat, and tears? Those who complete the race will likely affirm it is worth the reward. Those who opt out of the typical yearlong training program often disagree. What do an Ironman and the sport of scarcity have in common? The drive for success. Many of us who are overwhelmed live in a depleted state due to our own driven nature. While God wired us to be responsible and accountable for excellence, we twist those wires to believe we are less if we fail to achieve certain goals. We become driven by the race, rather than our purpose.

I drill through a mental exercise once a year where I ask myself, If I learned tomorrow that I had only six months to live, what would I invest my energies in? Am I succeeding in things that have long-term value or a short-term reward?

What about you? Try this exercise with me.

- Make a list of all the things you currently invest your time and energy in.

    Which of these have a lasting implication, and which are more temporal?

    What steps do you need to take to opt out of or reduce the time and energy you invest in the trivial?

- Now, make a new list.

    Can you add something that will help you grow your faith rather than detract from it?

    Can you add an opportunity to love and serve others better?

IT IS USELESS FOR YOU TO WORK SO HARD FROM EARLY MORNING UNTIL LATE AT NIGHT, ANXIOUSLY WORKING FOR FOOD TO EAT; FOR GOD GIVES REST TO HIS LOVED ONES.

PSALM 127:2

This devotion is in no way an indictment of those who have been called to participate in an Ironman; I only use this example because it, like so many things in our lives, is an incredibly demanding activity. The opening quote from D. L. Moody is one that challenges us to think. God gives us the free will to choose how we invest our hours and days, and what it is we chase after. It's our responsibility to discern if we're succeeding at things that truly matter in the long run.

DAY 53

COMPOUND EXERCISES

Multitasking is merely the opportunity to screw up
more than one thing at a time.
STEVE UZZELL

As I MENTIONED IN yesterday's devotion, I'm not an athlete. Today during my workout I struggled through an exercise that required the balance of a ballerina with the strength of a linebacker—of which I am neither.

But I am fond of these compound exercises for their efficiency. If you're not familiar with the process, a compound exercise is one that uses multiple muscle groups at one time. For example, as you deadlift on one leg with an eight-pound ViPR in tow, you're working the hamstrings, the glutes, the shoulders, and the abs all at the same time. And you know what that means. Bingo! I can get out of the gym in half the time. This is multitasking at its finest.

I once considered my ability to multitask a benefit to both myself and my employer; I was proud of the number of plates I could spin at one time. What I didn't realize until I was in my late forties was that this wasn't a gift at all; multitasking actually degraded the quality of my work product *and* my peace of mind. So, knowing this, why in the world, in my late fifties, would I attempt to write a book at the office as I work? In March of 2016, while running our marketing agency (which in itself is more than a full-time job), I began writing *Lord, Have Mercy: Help and Hope for Moms on Their Last Nerve*. With a July due date for my manuscript, I carefully plotted my timeline and carved out a couple of hours each day, along with a day and a half of writing on weekends.

Although the timeline was compressed, it felt totally achievable. And it was. Until the panic attacks started.

I knew what they were the minute they started. I recalled the first time these little heart palpitations *raced* onto the scene more than thirty years ago as I sat in a lecture class at college. At the time I was taking a fifteen-hour course load, working two part-time jobs, and raising two elementary-aged children. No doubt I was spread thin then, but now? Yes. Now. The amount of energy and focus required for me to dive deep into writing and then to abruptly pull out of that mind-set to answer questions from employees or clients was stressing my heart, mind, and soul. The constant back-and-forth was short-circuiting my brain.

I finally admitted to myself that I could do many things at once and have my work be shallow, or I could focus my energy on one thing for a short amount of time and go deep. So in writing this book, I reserved every Tuesday away from the office to focus only on you. Each morning began with a good workout, a hot shower (this is important to authors—we can go all day without bathing), and a steaming cup of joe, followed by an hour of prayer and study. After I was sufficiently filled and fueled, I began my "conversation" with you.

Sister,

- Could you reduce your stress by choosing to do fewer things at once?
- Do you take accountability for your schedule, or do you allow others to dictate it?
- What changes would you need to make to afford yourself some time for focused concentration?
- Would your attitude and relationships benefit or suffer because of this renewed dedication to focused quality work?

WHEN I AM OVERWHELMED, YOU ALONE KNOW THE WAY
I SHOULD TURN.

PSALM 142:3

During this devoted time of writing, I never opened e-mail. I didn't look at my phone. I didn't go shopping online or introduce any other distraction. I made sure it was just you, me, and the Father, Son, and Holy Spirit. And with that came a steady heart rate.

DAY 54

STRONG TIDES

Unless we stand for something, we shall fall for anything.
PETER MARSHALL

ONE MORNING, as we celebrated an anniversary in Cabo San Lucas, Mexico, Steve and I took off on a long, glorious morning stroll up the sandy beach. On the way back to our hotel, we happened upon a man taking a picture of his wife. I offered to take the couple's picture so they could have a visual record of that beautiful morning overlooking the Sea of Cortez. The husband offered to take our picture as well, so Steve and I turned to the camera with the sea at our backs. Our newfound photographer friend took our picture again and again—one after the next, from multiple angles as the tide began to rise without our knowledge. It rose so quickly, in fact, that the last picture captured the waves engulfing our feet and legs.

Laughing at the circumstance, we parted with the couple and thanked our photographer for his dedication to capturing the perfect shot (ha!), and Steve and I walked in fishy, smelly, soggy tennis shoes back up to our room. The lesson we learned that day: Don't stand with your back to a rising tide. (Steve insists the takeaway is "Don't let strangers take your picture.")

To excel in living the abundant life, we, too, must know where to stand on issues important to Christ. Relying on our own personal beliefs is like standing with our backs to the sea, waves rushing in—oblivious as to what's heading our way! Without a fully working knowledge of God's Word, our faith can either get knocked over or drown, or we can end up walking around as a smelly witness.

Being tolerant of those who walk outside the faith means only to love them unconditionally as God has commanded. It doesn't mean condoning sinful behavior, agreeing with a policy that is clearly in violation of God's laws, or apologizing for standing firm on our own principles of faith. In our "everything goes" society, we can easily find ourselves tossed about if we have not invested time and energy to learn God's truth because sometimes the lines begin to blur. As Charles Spurgeon so plainly stated, "Discernment is not knowing the difference between right and wrong. It is knowing the difference between right and almost right." In the end, God's Word is what will direct us and save us, while our own personal beliefs will leave us with little more than seaweed clinging to our socks.

Every day we face the strong cultural tides that roll in, and we must learn how to stand firmly planted on the beach. A few questions for you as you consider where you stand today:

- What guides you along your faith walk today—God's truth or your own personal beliefs?
- How do you stand against the cultural tide of tolerance?
- Does your witness sometimes get stinky?
- Or are you more apt to float along on the waves of "don't rock the boat," even if you know it's wrong?

TEACH ME YOUR WAY, LORD, THAT I MAY RELY ON YOUR FAITHFULNESS; GIVE ME AN UNDIVIDED HEART, THAT I MAY FEAR YOUR NAME.

PSALM 86:11, NIV

The sparkling sea looks inviting, and many are caught unawares as they float out on the tide. The good news: When they realize they're adrift, all they need to do is call on his name. Jesus saves.

DAY 55

PTO

Rest time is not waste time. It is economy to gather fresh strength. . . .
It is wisdom to take occasional furlough.
In the long run, we shall do more by sometimes doing less.
CHARLES SPURGEON

MANY ORGANIZATIONS REFER to vacation time as PTO, which stands for "personal time off" or "paid time off." But for some of us, this simply means we take our computers and smartphones poolside while the family plays without us. This action may seem harmless in the moment, but it is rocket fuel for the barren life and can cause the unraveling of personal, family, and professional success. Satan has tricked us into believing, along with our culture, that we must work harder and longer and be available every moment of every day, or we're a failure. It's a fact: According to the US Travel Association's Project: Time Off, more than half of Americans didn't take all their vacation days in 2015, up from 42 percent in previous years.[12]

I am protective of my PTO not because it is a thing to take or something to do but rather because it is the process for an outcome. For me, PTO stands for "Permit Transformation to Occur." Time away from work allows me to grant myself permission to embrace a total rest of mind, body, and spirit. Only then do I hear and understand what more I can do for God. During this time away from digital devices, conversations, and deadlines, I can finally hear and discern his calling.

Our society has fooled us into thinking we will get ahead only if we work longer and harder. Our employers have led us to believe we are less dedicated if we completely unplug. And we've convinced ourselves that the job will not get done without us. As a professional in the technology industry and a business owner, I'm here to say, hogwash! In fact, the opposite is true. Individuals and organizations flourish because of innovative ideas that result from a rested mind. Families are often renewed with dedicated and focused time far away from the constant interruptions of e-mail and texting. And our calling will be clear, our purpose fulfilled, and the abundant life that is promised will be realized when we finally permit transformation to occur.

Am I alone in this? How do you view PTO?

- Do you dread trying to juggle e-mails and conference calls on the beach while the rest of your family builds sand castles?
- Do you stay so busy on vacation that you have no time to rest and hear God's voice?
- Have you ever invited Jesus to come on vacation with you?
- What incredible professional and personal adventures might await you if you were to permit transformation to occur?

DON'T COPY THE BEHAVIOR AND CUSTOMS OF THIS WORLD, BUT LET GOD TRANSFORM YOU INTO A NEW PERSON BY CHANGING THE WAY YOU THINK. THEN YOU WILL LEARN TO KNOW GOD'S WILL FOR YOU, WHICH IS GOOD AND PLEASING AND PERFECT.

ROMANS 12:2

There was a time when I copied the behaviors of those around me, failing to embrace my PTO. I've even blown it a time or two, as you will read tomorrow! But I think I'm finally catching on: A rested heart, mind, and body are basic requirements for living a profitable, meaningful life. I'm cashing in my PTO.

DAY 56

JESUS SAVED YOU...
A CHAIR BY THE POOL

Come to me, all of you who are weary and carry heavy burdens,
and I will give you rest.
JESUS, Matthew 11:28

As WE PACKED OUR bags for our upcoming trip, Steve and I lamented that this particular vacation could not have come at a more inconvenient time. However, the trip to Santa Barbara and the central coast region of California with some of our dearest friends had been planned almost a year earlier. With deadlines looming on major projects, workplace issues swirling like a twister in May, and our home still under construction—and behind schedule—we boarded the plane anxious, exhausted, and emotionally burned out. You would think this would be the perfect time for us to rest and relax, but I couldn't do either. I was away from the problems physically, but that only added to my restless mental state.

Near the end of the vacation, our friends continued on along the California coast, and we stayed back in Santa Barbara for a few days. Deciding to spend the afternoon by the pool to enjoy the beautiful 75-degree day (all the more enjoyable knowing it was 110 degrees in Dallas), we settled in with books, magazines, a healthy supply of sunblock, and . . . our phones and notebook computers. Uh-oh. No personal transformation would be occurring this day!

Within the first half hour, I began a rapid exchange of e-mail with our employees as we dealt with a "crisis" that could have been addressed when I returned. Steve also hopped on e-mail and began to manage our construction project from fifteen hundred miles away. Two hours later, we closed our computers and turned off our phones, but by this point we were so frustrated, aggravated, and defeated that even the softly swaying palm trees couldn't unwind us. I closed my eyes and was immediately convicted: This was more than being poor stewards of our well-earned vacation. This was blatant disobedience.

In Matthew 11:28, "Come to me" is not a polite request. Jesus implores us, for our welfare, to move toward him and away from our trials and worldly distractions. "Who are weary and carry heavy burdens" is not a filler description but one that indicates Christ knows us intimately and wants to help relieve our challenges! And "I will give you rest" is not a hollow passing statement but a promise you can take to the bank. He's saved us a chair by the pool—one with soft fluffy towels, a refreshing beverage, and a beautiful view—but how often do we choose to sit in a hard, uncomfortable chair that faces a concrete wall, completely parched. And we wonder why we're spread too thin!

I'm curious. How did you spend your last PTO?

- Did you slather on the sunblock and get out your Bible or maybe close your eyes in meditation and prayer?
- Or waste most of the time behind a screen putting out fires at the office?

An affirmative answer to question one indicates you're living abundantly and obediently. Answering yes to question two reveals that even on vacation, you're spread too thin.

YOU CROWN THE YEAR WITH A BOUNTIFUL HARVEST;
EVEN THE HARD PATHWAYS OVERFLOW WITH ABUNDANCE.
PSALM 65:11

Your vacation is a blessing of the harvest that you have worked so hard to bring in. Jesus wants to celebrate with you—don't leave him sitting there alone.

DAY 57

LEARNING TO SIT ...
IN THE CHAIR BY THE POOL

Idleness is not just a vacation, an indulgence or a vice;
it is as indispensable to the brain as vitamin D is to the body, and
deprived of it we suffer a mental affliction as disfiguring as rickets. . . .
It is, paradoxically, necessary to getting any work done.

TIM KREIDER, "The 'Busy' Trap"

ONCE WE RECOGNIZE THAT Jesus has saved us that comfy chair by the pool and desires for us to join him, we need to learn to sit in it. This is a challenge for those of us who are naturally "busy."

If you've ever vacationed in Cabo San Lucas or a similar city, then you know that there are plenty of activities that can keep you entertained, from visiting one of the neighboring towns to joining excursions like whale watching or snorkeling. But after years of practice, I have finally learned a new sport at the beach: It's called sitting.

At the property where we frequently stay, it is not unusual that by midmorning, the "best seats in the house" (i.e., by the pool, looking out at the water) have been marked as reserved. Magazines, baseball caps, and towels lay claim to the premium chairs facing the Sea of Cortez. Here you can stare out at the ocean and, in February, watch mama whales splash and play with their calves. However, to take this in, you have to be willing to keep your eyes peeled straight ahead and simply sit. Unfortunately, due to our digital age, this is something many of us are not very good at doing.

I have found that to excel in "sitting," one must first learn the basic steps and then become disciplined in order to grow. The lesson begins with removing all materials and devices that distract the mind—this includes mobile phones, computers, music, and *even some books* (although a quick read of a good devotional is not all bad). Removing all forms of input or entertainment (beyond a whale show) benefits the mind. Think of your brain as a muscle group. If you were exercising your arms day in and day out by lifting large weights or carrying heavy pieces of furniture, over time your arms would become extremely fatigued. Our minds are the same way. While we're awake, our brains are always on, getting little time to rejuvenate, which impacts our creativity, the quality of our decision making, and our emotional stability.

It was during one of these distraction-free, mind-clearing moments when Steve and I sat in our beach chairs staring out at the vast ocean that he began to prod me about writing another book. *This* book, as a matter of fact. Together we began to explore various topics and the spiritual, emotional, mental, and physical benefits of trading in frantic living for lasting peace. As we both sat recovering from being spread too thin, this relaxed time allowed God to speak to us, resulting in *Spread Too Thin*.

A few questions for you today:

- When was the last time you simply sat?
- Would you be willing to relearn this ability if you've forgotten how?
- What do you think God might press on your heart if you allowed yourself this luxury?

TAKE MY YOKE UPON YOU. LET ME TEACH YOU, BECAUSE I AM HUMBLE AND GENTLE AT HEART, AND YOU WILL FIND REST FOR YOUR SOULS.
MATTHEW 11:29

When Christ said, "Take my yoke," he was asking us to be teachable. To be teachable, we must be reachable, and, yes, this means taking that seat beside him.

DAY 58

NO WORK ZONE

You have six days each week for your ordinary work, but
the seventh day is a Sabbath day of rest dedicated to the LORD your God.
GOD ALMIGHTY, Exodus 20:9-10

I RECENTLY SAW THE cutest office party decoration. It was yellow caution tape with the words "NO WORK ZONE" printed on it. The tape is used to prevent employees from accessing their work spaces while a social event is occurring at the office. I decided I might benefit from having a roll of this tape myself in order to block off my home office on Sundays.

You'd think that God Almighty's explicit direction (see the verse above) would be enough to motivate me to rest from my work at least *one* day a week. But I will tell you—because I have a full-time job and a family, I have managed to *justify* working seven days a week by internalizing that my writing and editing of devotionals is ministry and thus exempt. *Am I in marketing or what?*

Unfortunately, God is unlikely to be impressed by my attempt to justify my position. My "Sinful Sundays," as I refer to them, date back to the early 1990s when I allowed my workweek to begin on Sunday evening, rather than Monday morning. In those days, the retail world was driven by something called preprint—circulars that appeared in the Sunday morning newspaper. My upcoming challenges and opportunities were often determined by the success or failure of our advertising compared to our competitors', and to be prepared for our Monday morning staff meetings, I had to be informed. Regardless, this work wasn't biblical; it was merely cultural in our company and industry.

When God spoke to Moses in the verse above, he didn't specify that some job titles or tasks were exempt. Whether we're in ministry, writing code, or healing the sick, God has not requested but demanded that we rest and dedicate a full day (not just a morning) to him and our spiritual refreshment.

An abundant life is a fulfilling life, and a fulfilling life includes twenty-four hours of worship and rest. Whether you take your Sabbath on a weekday, Saturday, or Sunday is up to you. What you do with your Sabbath to grow in relationship with God is up to you too. Some questions to ponder today:

- Do you take a Sabbath every week?
- Do you sometimes try to sneak in a little bit of work?
- Is your rest or worship often interrupted when you do?
- Do you do this because you're overcommitted?
- Would you say what you're doing is more important than following God's commandment?
- Do you think God would say you're spread too thin?

GOD BLESSED THE SEVENTH DAY AND DECLARED IT HOLY, BECAUSE IT WAS THE DAY WHEN HE RESTED FROM ALL HIS WORK OF CREATION.

GENESIS 2:3

I've said it before and I'll say it again: If God the Father, creator of the heavens and earth, can afford to take a day off to rest, so must we.

DAY 59

START YOUR DAY WITH
A CUP OF JOE—AND
A POT OF FORGIVENESS

Always forgive your enemies; nothing annoys them so much.
OSCAR WILDE

I LOVE NOTHING MORE than waking up to a rich, steaming cup of coffee. For twenty-seven years, Steve has sweetly placed my "wake-up juice" on my bedside table as he's kissed me good morning. If you guessed that I am spoiled rotten by this man, you are correct, and if you jumped to the conclusion that I am rendered useless until that first shot of caffeine races through my veins, you are also spot on.

To live the uncommon life, we might not all need a cup of coffee or tea to get us going, but we all need a pot of forgiveness to get us through the day. Our Christian witness requires us to forgive quickly and even frequently. As living, breathing examples of Christ to the believer and unbeliever alike, we are held to a standard of nothing less than excellence when it comes to this often very difficult assignment.

If living out the abundant life requires a spirit of grace, it's pretty safe to say that withholding absolution propels a state of scarcity. Nothing will make one feel spread more thin emotionally than the bile of bitterness, the slow burn of anger, or floundering over hurt feelings. There's only one antidote: mercy given because of mercy received.

When I struggle with forgiving someone, I always go back to the New Testament story of the woman who had committed adultery. The

Pharisees, who were trying to trap Jesus, reminded him that the law of Moses called for her stoning, but Jesus had a different approach:

> Jesus bent down and started to write on the ground with his finger. When they kept on questioning him, he straightened up and said to them, "Let any one of you who is without sin be the first to throw a stone at her." Again he stooped down and wrote on the ground. At this, those who heard began to go away one at a time, the older ones first, until only Jesus was left, with the woman still standing there.
>
> JOHN 8:6-9, NIV

What do you think Jesus was writing in the dirt? Every sermon I have heard preached on this Scripture surmises that he was writing the sins of the men waiting to impart justice. I don't know about you, but I would die of embarrassment if Jesus walked in and began writing my sins on the whiteboard in our conference room. That idea coupled with Christ's sacrifice and his commandment to forgive as we have been forgiven has me refilling my pot of forgiveness first thing every morning. What about you?

- Are you forfeiting lasting peace because you're withholding forgiveness?
- Can extending mercy become a daily act for you in light of your own sins?
- Do you see how giving grace can advance the abundant life?

Life is so short, and we're all sinners. Even if we choose not to reconcile, we can elect to forgive. Animosity and a spirit of anger are sure to spread us all too thin.

DAY 60

THE NAKED LIZARD

The way to gain a good reputation is to endeavor to be what you desire to appear.
SOCRATES

STEVE AND I ONCE OWNED a home in a richly vegetated area of East Dallas. Our backyard, with its beautiful canopy of large trees and lush hedges, was almost forest-like. Only a few miles from the downtown area, we were still able to enjoy a nice variety of critters, from a mama raccoon and her triplets to a feral cat we fed and named Frankie. But that's not all. We also had naked lizards.

On the memory of my mammaw's fried chicken, I promise you I could see clean through those geckos. No more than four inches long, these little creatures were nearly transparent! I could see their bones and small blue patches under their skin. They were very strange. I was familiar with the two more common green lizards in our area that can change colors almost on cue, but you can imagine my surprise when I came eye to eye with this type of lizard that was, let's say, "exposed."

As Christians, either we can change our colors based on our need for acceptance and who we surround ourselves with, or we can be transparent. Unbelievers and Christians alike are often frustrated, confounded, or embarrassed when those who claim to be Jesus' disciples act in a way that is completely dishonoring to God. Masking our beliefs and blending in with society to the detriment of our witness is a breeding ground for scarcity because we will always be in conflict with our true selves. Today, for those of us who fail to live according to godly principles, the poor reflection is not just personal or a statement against our own character—our society views it as a poor reflection of Christ's church. Our beliefs and ideals as Christians should never intimidate others because we should engage with humility, thoughtfulness, and patience.

We need more naked lizards in our Bible studies and small groups, too. As fellow Christians, we are obligated to be real. The "perfect Christian" persona does nothing to build up the body of Christ. For those of us who have relied on the power of Christ to carry us through our trials, we serve as mentors and examples of an uncommon love and faith in Jesus Christ. When we share our past experiences, we become ministers of his love. When we're paralyzed with fear, crushed by disappointment, or experiencing loneliness and sorrow, our transparency is needed to invite the prayers of the righteous. Our humility and vulnerability are an example to others. And most importantly, our girlfriends can't pray for us if they don't know what's going on.

As believers, we must live as the naked lizards, not as those who will change their colors or markings to blend in. We are exposed—and because of that, our Savior is also laid bare. His reputation to a lost world often depends on our own. *No pressure.*

Only one question for you today because this is a pass/fail topic:

o Are you naked or not?

LIKE THE HOLY ONE WHO CALLED YOU, BE HOLY YOURSELVES.
1 PETER 1:15, NASB

Once I became accustomed to seeing that little critter's blue spots, I became rather fond of him. Others may find that it's intriguing to see what's inside us, too.

DAY 61

COMPETING MASTERS:
HOMEWORK AND HOME WORK

A "harmonized" life these days sounds like a tall order.
Between housework, homework, workwork, and busywork,
there are perpetually too many things to do, and not enough time to find
that mythical balance. Nothing is more frustrating than feeling like you're
doing doing doing but getting nothing truly done that you really want.

JACK CANFIELD

"A HARMONIZED LIFE" IS definitely not the description our daughter, Shauna, would use at her current life stage. "Living the dream," she has a demanding job and boss, a husband whose career requires frequent travel, a neighbor who wants to argue over a fence that was put in three inches over their property line by the previous owners, an English bulldog with irritable bowel syndrome, and an eight-year-old daughter who's gone toe-to-toe with her every night for the past two weeks over a book report. Driving the car pool, doing laundry, grocery shopping, getting dinner on the table, attending soccer games, and teaching Sunday school are just a few of the other masters competing for her attention that have her spread too thin. Sound familiar to you? I bet it does, especially if you have *multiple* kids. Your day is this times three! Oh, God bless you, sweet mothers!

If there's any demographic among us that is hanging on by a thread, it's our working moms. I think about you all very often and pray for you, as I expressed in my book *Lord, Have Mercy: Help and Hope for Moms on Their Last Nerve*. While it was definitely challenging for my generation as we worked and raised children, it was neither as complex, as rushed, or as exhausting as it is today. But I have found a treasure buried in Scripture for those of you who long to conquer frantic living produced by all your demands:

> MY DEAR BROTHERS AND SISTERS, BE STRONG AND IMMOVABLE.
> ALWAYS WORK ENTHUSIASTICALLY FOR THE LORD, FOR YOU
> KNOW THAT NOTHING YOU DO FOR THE LORD IS EVER USELESS.
>
> 1 CORINTHIANS 15:58

Consider this verse and align your day and attitude with the phrase "Nothing you do *for the Lord* is ever useless." Clearly, we can—and often do—expend a tremendous amount of energy on activities and issues that are not of great value, and it's those things that drain us and spread us too thin. But what we take on enthusiastically, specifically for God's glory, are the building blocks of an abundant life.

So here's an exercise for you. Write down what's going on in your life that requires an exorbitant amount of mental, emotional, physical, and/or spiritual energy (I hope I've allowed you enough space):

Now, cross off everything that consumes you and will likely have no lasting benefit beyond the next thirty days. Then circle those things that are eternal in nature. Do with enthusiasm what's not crossed off and give God the glory as you perform them. Voilà. You may still be a bit overwhelmed, but hopefully you're also overwhelmed with the promise of purpose. A funny side note: That fussy neighbor who spread Shauna way too thin suddenly moved. Drama gone, just like that. What a great reminder that God has a sense of humor and that those things that often weigh us down will be resolved in his time and in his own perfect way.

DAY 62

COMPETING MASTERS:
CHICKEN POX AND
PURCHASE ORDERS

I think while all mothers deal with feelings of guilt,
working mothers are plagued by guilt on steroids!
ARIANNA HUFFINGTON

THERE WAS NO question in my mind; I was staying home. The year was 1991. Scott had just come off a two-week bout of the chicken pox when Shauna's first pocks began to appear. At fourteen, she had contracted the more serious form of the illness and was terribly sick. For days I lay with her on the sofa, stroking her head, wondering if at any moment we were headed for the ER (and checking frequently for signs of my first marks too!). I had been home from work for more than three weeks. Unlike the flexibility of working remotely that some of us enjoy today, my work was piling up, and my contributions to my team were sorely missed. As the date for the largest trade show in our industry loomed closer and closer, I became more and more stressed—worried sick for my daughter's health and worried sick that I was about to be fired.

Although there was no question that I was staying home, there was no doubt that I had to go to the trade show. I had only been with my company and in my role as a buyer for six months. Held in Las Vegas each year, this trade show was the most important buying event of the year—one where major deals were negotiated and allocation for the next season's product was committed. To fulfill my most basic obligation to my employer, I absolutely had to be there. When the phone rang a week before the opening day of the event, I held my breath as my boss asked, "So, are you coming?" Swallowing hard, I apologetically explained, "I still don't know. My daughter is still very sick, and I can't possibly leave her in this condition."

I was overwhelmed—navigating waters I had not traversed before. I felt a heavy burden for not being available to my company, an incredible guilt for even wanting to attend the show (this was a big deal for my career), an even greater guilt for having the fleeting thought that I might be able to go, and heartbreak for my sweet, sick, polka-dotted daughter. I spent a solid ten days in a state of fear and anxiousness.

This is a dilemma I suspect many of you moms have likely faced or are currently facing—the intellectual and heartfelt responsibility of doing your job to the best of your ability while fulfilling your first and foremost role as a mother or caregiver. The competing masters nearly do you in, and you find yourself spread too thin both physically and emotionally. Where does this devotion find you today?

- Do the competing masters of obligation to your employer and care for your family (children or aging parents) burden you?
- When you recognize this strain, guilt, or fear, how do you manage it?
- Do you struggle with the guilt of not being able to be all things to all people all the time?

DON'T PANIC. I'M WITH YOU. THERE'S NO NEED TO FEAR FOR I'M YOUR GOD. I'LL GIVE YOU STRENGTH. I'LL HELP YOU. I'LL HOLD YOU STEADY, KEEP A FIRM GRIP ON YOU.
ISAIAH 41:10, MSG

Job or no job, my sweet treasure of a daughter was coming first. But the day before the start of the trade show, I called my boss and told him excitedly that I would be joining him and the team in Las Vegas. The Great Healer provided—just in the nick of time. Shauna turned the corner, and I kept my job. And I didn't come down with the chicken pox for another couple of years. But that's a story for my next book.

DAY 63

COMPETING MASTERS: SERVING MAN AND SERVING *THE* MAN

Faithful servants never retire. . . . You can retire from your career,
but you will never retire from serving God.

RICK WARREN

IF YOU PICKED UP THIS book because of its title, there's a good chance that you are overextended in some way. If you're involved in ministry, active in your church, or a dedicated volunteer to your community, then there's a good chance that if not today, at some point in the future you may experience the physical, mental, and spiritual conflict of ministry or volunteer burnout. I'm speaking, of course, from experience.

Spinning too many plates—even when the work is profitable for both you and the organization—can leave you empty. I didn't know this when I was young; I could have used a mentor to help me see that the ministries I volunteered with and my overall work were good and noble but not always glorifying. No one told me that one day the resulting burnout might even become a hindrance to my future service.

Overserving in a community, church, or school can lead to a depleted spirit. Even when we love our work or assignment, challenges often surface, including conflicts of time and increased demands of our energy or resources—all of which can cause our passion to wane. This leads to the worst possible scenario: an exhausted servant's heart. Sis, we have to recognize that when we have the competing masters of serving man and serving God in play, we must proactively choose God for the sake of our greater good and for his glory.

Taking a sabbatical from service is not a cop-out. When we recognize our struggle to serve enthusiastically or with a spirit of love, we need to speak up and take a break. Serving God is not a sprint but a lifelong marathon. The saddest thing in the world is to tire yourself out today and have nothing to give tomorrow.

Answer honestly for yourself:

- I am only serving out of obligation. My heart is not passionate about my service.
- I would like to retire from my position, but I'm embarrassed to quit.
- God expects me to work and serve him, even if I'm exhausted and doing my job poorly.
- I would feel so refreshed and energized to step down from _____(this one board, this one committee, teaching this class).
- If I could turn back time, I would only be involved in _____ because I know it is my calling, serves God with my gifts, and is done with an enthusiastic heart.

WHATEVER YOU DO, WORK AT IT WITH ALL YOUR HEART, AS WORKING FOR THE LORD, NOT FOR HUMAN MASTERS, SINCE YOU KNOW THAT YOU WILL RECEIVE AN INHERITANCE FROM THE LORD AS A REWARD. IT IS THE LORD CHRIST YOU ARE SERVING.

COLOSSIANS 3:23-24, NIV

Our inheritance as followers of Christ includes an abundant life on earth, walking more closely with our Savior, having access to his power over Satan, and having his peace in the midst of crisis. This list of treasures, of course, goes on and on. Lay claim to your inheritance as you serve God, remembering that service doesn't save—and if performed in the wrong spirit can even harm. Take a break if you need it. Then ask God to lead you only where your gifts will bring glory to his Kingdom. There's no retirement from serving God. He has work for you to do.

DAY 64

THE TABATA OF SERVICE

Never tire of doing even the smallest things for Him, because He isn't impressed so much with the dimensions of our work as with the love in which it is done.
BROTHER LAWRENCE, *The Practice of the Presence of God*

TO THE EXTENT ONE CAN *enjoy* doing push-ups at 6:00 a.m., I enjoy my morning workouts. Or at least I did until today. Upon my arrival, Lisa (my trainer) bounced in with a sunny smile and asked, "Do you want to do something fun today? Have you ever done Tabata?"

"Ta-*who*?" I replied. Less than three minutes into the drill, I knew more about this exercise philosophy than I ever wanted to learn. This training shouldn't be called Tabata but Ta-BAD-a. A quick overview for those of you who haven't had the *joy* of experiencing this for yourselves: It's interval training in which you perform a particular exercise for twenty seconds, followed by a ten-second rest. You do the same exercise eight times on the same leg or with the same arm and then switch. I'm with you—it didn't sound difficult when my trainer explained it, but I kid you not, delivering Shauna Lynn after twenty-four hours of labor was less exhausting.

I slowly walked home from the gym, struggling to put one foot in front of the other. Stepping into the shower, I could barely raise my arms to wash my hair. I sit at this moment, four hours postworkout, with my feet propped up on a chair because it takes too much energy to sit up straight. I'm *still* exhausted.

And yet I know this exhaustion will eventually go away, unlike the endless exhaustion that many of you out there face. I believe that caring for family members who are in need—from raising grandchildren to caring for adult children with special needs to seeing your parents through their final years—is the Tabata of service. It is physically exhausting, profoundly mind-numbing, intensely frustrating, and completely heartbreaking. You want to cry (because everything seems so unfair); you want to scream, "I'm not doing this anymore" (as you deal with grown children with addiction); you want your sick, cranky, forgetful parents to go back to the healthy, sweet, kind people you've always known them to be; and for some of you, you want to spoil those sweet little grandkids rotten, but you can't. Stepping into the role of being their parent or guardian, you're now the one on their case to get their homework done. These are just a few examples of the Tabata of service.

For those of you reading this who are spread too thin from the daily demands of caring for family members, I want you to know that God sees and is glorified by your sacrifice. He understands this season of Tabata and the love through which you serve, even in the most frustrating and defeating of days. He isn't surprised by the circumstances or that you have shown up to sweat through the details of care. Like my Tabata session, your season of service has likely made you stronger, humbler, and all the more determined to serve with grace.

If this book falls into your hands while you are spread too thin from caring for your parents, adult children in need, or grandchildren, let me ask you,

- Are you completely exhausted?
- Do you feel angry or emotionally spent?
- Do you feel bad that you feel bad about this season of care?
- Have you gone to Christ for refreshment?
- Is it easier to face tomorrow knowing that he is glorified by the love in which you serve?

JESUS SAID, "COME TO ME, ALL OF YOU WHO ARE WEARY AND CARRY HEAVY BURDENS, AND I WILL GIVE YOU REST."
MATTHEW 11:28

When my body has fully recovered from my Tabata training session, I will truly say I am joyful (because it's over). For those of you who are strained by the daily grind of your Tabata service, I pray you will see how God delights in your sacrifice. Large or small, for a few weeks or years or maybe for a lifetime—you are blessing your family and him.

DAY 65

HONESTLY, IT'S THE KIDS

*Someday my children will look fondly on the annoying things I did
and see them clearly as evidence of love.*

RICHELLE E. GOODRICH,
Making Wishes: Quotes, Thoughts, & a Little Poetry for Every Day of the Year

IF YOU'RE A MOM, there's a good chance that on any given day you feel completely washed up, wrung out, and hung up to dry. Few things can spread a woman more thin than her cherubs.

One of the best parenting books ever written is found about halfway through the Bible. The book of Proverbs is a classic for direction and correction, providing straightforward advice to children as to how they should behave and to parents as to how they can *encourage* their kiddos to behave. I love that God so "gets us" that he inspired Solomon and some other really wise guys to provide us solid counsel as well as spiritual and emotional "backup." God knew before we did that those cute little boogers can bankrupt our emotional, mental, and physical accounts before their morning snacks—*if* we give them the power to make such a withdrawal.

The tug-of-war waged between a mom and her three-year-old often feels like a power struggle; by the time the child is a teenager, it *is* a power struggle, as he or she searches for identity and independence to begin their separation from Mom. But the battle for autonomy that is fought while the child is young—the one that spreads many a mommy too thin—can be contained when limits are placed in two key areas: negotiation and complaining.

A recent visit with a veteran teacher of thirty years confirmed something I had suspected: This generation of children is more capable and thus more confident to debate with figures of authority. As a grandmother of a very bright fourth grader, I think this ability to engage with and question superiors stems from their advanced language skills compared to that of previous generations. Their understanding that many things are negotiable is well established by the time they're two; by the age of three, they have honed those skills to the point that they believe *everything* is negotiable. They have learned what many of us who excel in negotiations know—all they need to do is hold out. Sooner or later, they will wear the opponent down. So here's a tip from a woman who has negotiated for a living: When you stop, they stop. No one can counter if you don't. They must know that some things—from what's for dinner to doing homework *now* to challenging authority—are nonnegotiable.

When my children were young, I can honestly say I don't remember either of them seriously complaining until they hit the seventh grade. During those teen years as hormones rage, demands of school increase, and the waters of social circles become more muddied, it is expected that they will become irritable and frustrated with the world. But a six-year-old living in the suburbs of the United States of America? What in the Sam Hill do most of our children have to complain about? But unfortunately more and more children have found this to be a successful path to spreading their moms too thin. If they complain long enough, loud enough, and with a bit of drama, sooner or later Mom will succumb because she's too worn out to enforce rules, have them complete their chores, and turn off the video games. They win. Temporarily. But in the long run, they lose because they've mastered the sin of complaining.

If you're a mom, these questions are for you:

o Where do you go for your parenting advice?
o Have you read Solomon's wise words that were written to uplift and rescue the weary souls of parents?

- Do you need to stop negotiating?
- Do you need to put an end to your child's complaining?

POINT YOUR KIDS IN THE RIGHT DIRECTION—WHEN THEY'RE
OLD THEY WON'T BE LOST.
PROVERBS 22:6, MSG

Embrace their individuality. Celebrate their confidence. Engage them in dynamic, profitable conversation. But don't let those adorable cherubs make one more withdrawal from your emotional and mental bank account.

DAY 66

TO BE COMPLETELY HONEST,
IT'S *THAT* KID

So why in heaven, even when I pointed him in the right direction,
did he head south?

ELLEN MILLER

IF MY QUESTION APPEARS to challenge Proverbs 22:6 (yesterday's verse), it's not meant to. It's just my human response to a spiritual dilemma. I have asked this question a thousand times over the years, and one night Christ all but whispered to me, "Ellen, you can be responsible for what is in front of you but not for the unseen. There are circumstances and forces beyond *your* control."

Parenting a regular kid (note I didn't use the word *normal*—are any of them normal?) is trying—especially during those confusing and often painful teenage and young adult years. But there is nothing more heartbreaking and gut-wrenching than parenting a child with challenges.

Eating disorders. Self-injury. Depression. Addiction. Autism. Schizophrenia. These are but a handful of challenging conditions and diseases that have one commonality: They're often inherited. Our ancestral gene pool is teeming with things we can't see or prepare for. Out of the blue, a once happy, delightful, healthy child can take an abrupt turn, morphing into a person we no longer recognize. A complete stranger now lies on our sofa.

We spread ourselves thin trying to rationalize with an irrational mind, coax an unwilling participant, or bargain with a child who sometimes feels like a traitor and disrupter to the family unit. Intellectually, we know our child's illness has taken control, but spiritually and emotionally, we still grapple with "What did *we* do wrong?" or "Why can't *they* snap out of this?" In desperation, we try *everything*. In some cases, the child receives healing and success through treatment centers, medications, and counseling; however, in many cases, no relief is found. We watch our child being pulled beneath the waters, and we pray for God to help us extend our hand further beneath the surface to pull him or her out. But time and time again our grasp falls short. My sweet sister, I know what it is like to be spread thin by a child who is challenged by an unrelenting gene pool.

However, just as we know that our child never chose to have these issues or conditions, we can neither give up nor allow him or her to succumb to them. I have a predisposition to high cholesterol and osteo-porosis. Knowing these conditions are in my genes, I have a responsibility to limit my hamburgers and do weight-bearing exercises to strengthen my bones. There's nothing my parents did that caused me these defects other than give me life. And knowing that they're just risks—not guarantees—doesn't let me off the hook to take action toward them myself.

If you're currently in this boat and watching your child struggle, there is one place and one place only I know to find the strength to retain your own sanity through these difficult times—and that is in the love, faith, and fellowship of Jesus Christ. Your child may not conform to your teaching or to the truth and hope found in Christ, but you can. Actually, to get through this heart-wrenching time and live abundantly, you must.

Let me ask you, mom to mom:

o Have you ever asked, "What did we do wrong?"
o If your child is straying from his or her faith, have you wondered why this is happening when you worked so hard to raise him or her according to the teachings of Christ?
o Have you blamed your children for their challenges?
o Do you let them off the hook because their illness or addiction is in their genes?

WHEN I WALK INTO THE THICK OF TROUBLE, KEEP ME ALIVE IN
THE ANGRY TURMOIL. WITH ONE HAND STRIKE MY FOES, WITH
YOUR OTHER HAND SAVE ME. FINISH WHAT YOU STARTED IN ME,
GOD. YOUR LOVE IS ETERNAL—DON'T QUIT ON ME NOW.
PSALM 138:7-8, MSG

Another condition that should be added to the list is cancer. If you
can relate to a mother who is losing her child to this battle, I hope you
can relate to mothers who are fighting on their own fronts. All are illnesses. All can bankrupt lasting peace.

DAY 67

TO THINE OWN SELF BE TRUE

Have enough sense to know, ahead of time,
when your skills will not extend to wallpapering.

MARILYN VOS SAVANT

IN 1985, I WAS A YOUNG MOTHER on a very tight budget, living with the most hideous kitchen wallpaper you've ever seen in your life. It was yellow and green with little people and houses "cross-stitched" all over it. I can honestly say it was atrocious. After listening to a couple of friends talk about how they replaced their wallpaper, I decided I should do the same. Unfortunately, I had no idea that I could not hang wallpaper—until the day I tore the old paper off. My kitchen disaster ended in tears, arguments, chaos, unexpected expenses, and shock: *How could I not hang wallpaper?* It looked so easy.

Trying something new is good for both the body and mind but is often more fruitful when we have the God-given gifts or associated skills to build from. When we strive to do something that is not in our wheelhouse, or perhaps in God's plan for us, we can find ourselves spread way too thin.

During my first two years of college, I majored in piano. During this time, I taught classical piano and could play very well. But I had neither the God-given talent nor the aptitude to be truly excellent. Unfortunately, no one told me this; I had to discern this on my own by comparing my skills to others as objectively as I could and visiting with my professors. It was hard and discouraging because I had worked and practiced toward this goal for nearly twenty years. But when I gave up on the thing I aspired so hard to be, I fell into the profession and work that came with so much more reward for my effort.

Friend, I know you're working very hard whether you are naturally gifted at your work or not. But the difference is, the hard work for which you're naturally gifted will be profitable, providing you with optimism, enthusiasm, and accomplishment—replacing those feelings of anxiousness, dread, and disorder that might have you spread too thin.

A few questions for you to consider:

- Are you working harder than ever, yet you're completely drained and never fulfilled by your work?
- Have you been repeatedly overlooked for promotions or appointments to boards and committees?
- Could God be calling you to another line of work or service for which he has blessed you with the gifts and aptitude you need to thrive?

SHE GOES TO INSPECT A FIELD AND BUYS IT; WITH HER EARNINGS SHE PLANTS A VINEYARD. SHE IS ENERGETIC AND STRONG, A HARD WORKER. SHE MAKES SURE HER DEALINGS ARE PROFITABLE; HER LAMP BURNS LATE INTO THE NIGHT.

PROVERBS 31:16-18

That Proverbs 31 woman sounds too good to be true, but she was. It's not that she was perfect, she was just a good steward of the talents she had been given. Nowhere does it say that she was great at hanging wallpaper.

DAY 68

MISSED EXPECTATIONS

When you own your choices, you own their consequences.

JACK WELCH

SOME OF US SUFFER FROM an affliction that I call the "next shiny thing." Our attention is diverted from the task at hand to new opportunities, or we allow ourselves to be distracted by an onslaught of incoming e-mails, texts, media campaigns, news articles, and the like. With a thousand things coming at us that may seem interesting or important, it's easy to get distracted from the few things that truly matter.

To accomplish those few things that God has purposed me to do, there are things I don't do, even though I know I'd like to. I am not the friend who sends birthday cards or calls frequently. I am not the first to raise my hand when a volunteer role needs to be filled or a service needs to be performed. It's not that I can't be a more available friend or citizen, it's that I've had to come to terms with my limits. I know that I cannot be all things to all people or even be the one thing that some people expect. It's taken me more than five decades to understand that I must focus on what I know I am called to do. I have prioritized my service and almost every daily act around one goal: not missing *his* expectation.

Doing a few things with excellence for Christ is hard to manage when other beautiful, lovely people and opportunities to serve are available to us. But if we don't proactively manage our time and give ourselves a pass to put Christ first (and everyone else in their proper priority order), we can find that our mental, physical, and emotional energy drains away.

One of my favorite Bible stories that depicts the importance of keeping our purpose focused is that of Nehemiah. The long story short is that

Nehemiah had been called to a special project—doing God's work to oversee the rebuilding of the wall around Jerusalem. Just as we're used to in work settings, there was controversy, and a few of Nehemiah's enemies saw this wall as a threat to their power. Shocking, right? Over the course of months, these men did everything they could to distract, antagonize, and deter Nehemiah—to the point of threatening him and his team. After a while, they tried a different tactic. They wanted Nehemiah to stop his work and meet with them in a plain, in the middle of nowhere, more than twenty miles away, but Nehemiah remained focused on what he was called to do and replied to them—not once but four times—

I AM DOING A GREAT WORK AND I CANNOT COME DOWN.
NEHEMIAH 6:3, NRSV

Nehemiah knew that to accomplish this very significant calling, he had to rely on God. He had to continuously pray and trust that God would provide for him. Can you imagine what we would all accomplish if we focused on what we're called to do rather than give our attention to the next shiny thing or passing interruption?

A few questions for you to determine whether you've established boundaries to fulfill your calling:

○ Do short-term distractions and meaningless "minor emergencies" keep you from doing great work?
○ Is every person you've ever loved and cared for number one on your priority list?
○ Do others instill feelings of guilt in you when you're unavailable to them according to their expectations versus your calling?
○ What would you accomplish if you could adopt a Nehemiah mind-set?

As an aside, Nehemiah means "comforter." Imagine the comfort we would all have if we could focus on our "wall" and not the distractions that keep us from our most essential endeavor.

DAY 69

HOW ARE YOU HOLDING UP?

THERE'S A LOT PULLING AT US—some of which will contribute to abundant living, but as we all know, there are circumstances, opportunities, and challenges that can wipe us out. We all long to live a deeply meaningful life and desire to spend our days profitably, but to do so, we have to make choices to keep us going for the long run. D. L. Moody's quote on day 52 is one of my favorites—one that I use to measure my choices: "Our greatest fear should not be of failure, but of succeeding at something that doesn't really matter." What clarity! As we bring this section to a close, may I ask you,

- Have you made decisions or commitments that will equip you for the long run?
- Have you prioritized your rest in order to serve with excellence?
- Have you created margin in your life in the areas of money, time, and forgiveness?
- Have you prayed about attitudes or choices that have you spread thin?
- Are you succeeding in things that don't really matter to the detriment of what does?

HOLY GOD, CREATOR OF HEAVEN AND EARTH,

We praise you with our hearts and voices. We lift our prayers of adoration to you for the loving, generous Father you are.

We confess that we are easily pulled by the tides of this world, forsaking you and your truth. We beg for your forgiveness in light of our past failures to forgive, understanding that this behavior negates the abundant life you long for us to enjoy. We are ashamed that we have not invested more time to know you through the study of your Word, even as we fall at your feet in times of crisis. We know we often live on the edge of time, money, and energy and repent of our multitasking that we might be available to serve when you call.

Although we serve multiple masters, we thank you, Father, for the opportunities you afford us and the people you provide us to serve. We are blessed beyond measure for the richness of our relationships and for every candle you give us to light for someone else. For the promise of lasting peace and the revelation of what fuels our frantic living, holy Father, we thank you.

We call upon your power to give us a heart for excellence that will bring honor to you. Kindle our passion for the purpose you've ordained us to. Convict us to be better stewards of rest so that we will be prepared to live more high-impact days for your glory. We pray you will be pleased as we strive to serve in love and live holy and wholly, for you.

In the name of the Father, the Son, and the Holy Spirit we pray. Amen.

PART 4

SOUL
SEARCHING
for the
ABUNDANT
LIFE

DAY 70

BLACKOUT SHADES

The vigor of our spiritual life will be in exact proportion to the place held by the Bible in our life and thoughts.

GEORGE MUELLER

STEVE AND I WERE SUFFERING from jet lag as a result of our overnight flight to Spain and the seven-hour time difference. We fell into bed around 4:00 a.m., exhausted but excited to be on vacation. Our intent was to take a three-hour nap. As early risers, we always awaken long before our alarm goes off, and being on vacation, we saw no need to set one. But when I began to stir awake that morning, I rolled over and groggily looked at the clock, then yelled to Steve, "Get up! It's 11:30!" I ran to the window, raised the blackout shades, and was blinded by the nearly noonday sunlight. We had no earthly idea that we had slept halfway through our first day of vacation *and* missed the "free" breakfast that was included with our reservation package.

But even worse than sleeping through precious hours of a vacation is sleeping through the abundant life. Many of us can completely miss out on this gift, due to either a lack of solid biblical teaching or a wandering away from Christ. Maybe our shades have been pulled down by apathy, or we're in the dark due to waywardness, or we have allowed our pride and self-reliance to block out the Son.

As the light flooded our room, Steve and I sprang to life from our almost comatose sleep as if hit by a jolt of electricity. Although we had both been waking up on and off for hours, because of the total darkness we had convinced ourselves it was still night. We were wrong; our minds were deceiving us. And like that first lost morning of our glorious vacation, you and I can find ourselves sleepwalking through the abundant life if we don't choose to raise our blinds to the Light.

To live the life Christ has promised requires soul-searching, and to do that we're going to have to roll over, put our two feet on the floor, and walk over to our Bible. To let the light in, we'll need to open it, read it, and meditate on what we have learned. To adopt the abundant life, we'll need to reconsider what distracts and deters us from growth and fruitfulness, and what lies are fueling our sense of scarcity. Here's where a good church and a small group Bible study come into play. God's holy Word, his guidance, and the support of other godly women will awaken us from our dreamy slumber, but, sweet sister, first we have to open our eyes.

The last section of this devotional will expose us further to the truth, God's promises, and his longing for a relationship with us. Knowing and understanding his Word better each day should be a wake-up call for us all. Let me ask,

- Are you sleeping through the abundant life?
- Have you dismissed the need for or wandered away from a deeper study of God's Word?
- Will you raise your blinds with me?

BY YOUR WORDS I CAN SEE WHERE I'M GOING; THEY THROW A BEAM OF LIGHT ON MY DARK PATH. I'VE COMMITTED MYSELF AND I'LL NEVER TURN BACK FROM LIVING BY YOUR RIGHTEOUS ORDER. EVERYTHING'S FALLING APART ON ME, GOD; PUT ME TOGETHER AGAIN WITH YOUR WORD.
PSALM 119:105-107, MSG

Without the Son shining in on us, we can sleepwalk through life and be oblivious to the fabulous inheritance Jesus has promised. Girlfriend, we end up missing out on a whole lot more than free breakfast.

DAY 71

A YEAR OF SECOND DATES

We must know before we can love.
In order to know God, we must often think of him.
BROTHER LAWRENCE, *The Practice of the Presence of God*

BEFORE OUR FIRST DATE, Steve and I conducted business together for about a year—over the phone! During those months we became acquainted with each other's temperament, wit, and resourcefulness as we solved business challenges together. I call this the year of second dates because it was the time in which we truly got to know one another. By the time of our *first* date, we had already enjoyed a year of discovering things about each other based on knowledge, not emotion. Our ongoing dates continued to reveal things to me, and my admiration gave way to adoration. But before I grew to love Steve, I had to know him. And so it is with God.

Many a woman has shared with me her fear of her creator—and not a fear born out of respect. Some have disclosed to me their distrust of the Father. A few have looked at me with searching eyes, confessing they don't know if our God is a God of love, and some people have told me (albeit politely) that they could never believe. All four mind-sets have two factors in common: limited biblical knowledge and limited understanding of grace.

Reading the Bible and learning the facts helps us to know God. From Genesis to Revelation, we uncover a God who is not angry but patient, and we discover a Father who adores his children like no other. He's created everything for us and desires to bless us with all that is good. From the gift of our earthly life to the sacrifice of his Son for our eternal salvation, this is a God who is not to be distrusted, but one who can always be counted on. He may not always give us what we want, but he always provides those things that are excellent for us and for his glory. He is not a God to be suspicious of or frightened by. Oh yes, he *is* a jealous God; he wants me to love only him, just as my Steve expects that I love only him as my husband. But God does not chasten us for our lack of fidelity to him; instead he gently but persistently calls us toward him.

My commitment to Steve hasn't imprisoned me—instead my love for him has freed me to be who I am meant to be. Loving God is not restricting either; it is a freedom unlike any other. And it's more; it's a partnership. Whether Steve and I are walking through a crisis together or skipping through our happiest of days, I love him the same. And as with God, the deeper we come to abide in him and to intimately know him, "we will learn to love him equally in times of distress or in times of great joy."[13]

These questions may be the most important that I ask you:

o How well do you know God?
o Is your assessment of God one that you arrived at on your own through personal study, or have others influenced your opinion?
o Is your study well grounded in the Word of God, or do you rely on the conclusions drawn by others in books and articles?
o If you rely on the conclusions drawn by others, how can you be sure these people know God?

WHAT MARVELOUS LOVE THE FATHER HAS EXTENDED TO US! JUST LOOK AT IT—WE'RE CALLED CHILDREN OF GOD! THAT'S WHO WE REALLY ARE. BUT THAT'S ALSO WHY THE WORLD DOESN'T RECOGNIZE US OR TAKE US SERIOUSLY, BECAUSE IT HAS NO IDEA WHO HE IS OR WHAT HE'S UP TO.

1 JOHN 3:1, MSG

The abundant life begins and ends with a deep, abiding love for God. This love, in itself, is the antidote for a life spread too thin. But first we have to know him to love him.

DAY 72

THE DAY DATE

What love and what mercy! What infinite grace!
Christ Jesus was willing to die in our place.
Then God sent the Spirit to convict us of sin,
To make us new creatures and abide then within.

J. C. O'HAIR, "The God of All Grace"

AFTER A YEAR OF "SECOND DATES," Steve asked me out on a first date—an evening affair of dinner and jazz (so sophisticated!). Adding to my previous understanding of his temperament, wit, and resourcefulness, I discovered this man had a wide variety of interests, was incredibly intelligent, and possessed the most gentlemanly ways. As we enjoyed our conversation over plates of pasta, I thought to myself, *This is a guy I can hang out with. I can see us being friends forever.* After he walked me to my front door at the end of the evening, I uncovered something else about Steve I hadn't known: He was an awesome kisser. What a great trait to have in a "friend"! (Things were looking up for Ellen!)

Two weeks later, we ventured out on a day date—twelve uninterrupted hours of togetherness would certainly be enlightening, one way or the other. As we walked through a museum, talked over lunch, and took in sights around the city, we each carefully peeled back, layer by layer, the complexity of the other human being. To know a person fully, we have to go deep.

Once we come to know God and begin to understand his unconditional love for us, there's another really complex aspect of his character to unwrap, explore, and adopt. And that is his grace. In our dog-eat-dog world, the ideology of grace is *really* hard for many of us to grasp because we so rarely experience it. Instead our interactions are more often punctuated by agitation, disappointment, and anger. Having not seen grace modeled ourselves, many of us do not know how to offer it or even respond when it crosses our paths. But grace is this: an unearned gift of mercy, pardon, and favor. It's that simple. It's a gift we've been given by God, not because of anything we've done, but because of *who* God is—a loving Father who forgives us repeatedly, never punishes us as we deserve, and gives us everything that he can for our good. That's how much he loves us. How can we *not* love him back?

God's character is best learned from pastors and Bible teachers who are well educated and called by God to bear witness to this love. Just as I would not entrust a friend to inform me on how to perform my own tooth extraction, I also don't look for friends to guide me in my quest of knowledge about God. My friend can recommend her dentist and share with me her best tips for oral hygiene, but when it comes to treating a major toothache—I'm looking for a specialist! And so it is with my spiritual maturation.

Truth is found in knowledge, not opinion that can be formed by errant thinking. When we discover this truth of God's grace and love, we realize our creator is not vindictive, angry, disinterested, or deceitful. We uncover just the opposite: He is forgiving, patient, engaged, and faithful. May I ask you to explore this truth with me today?

- Have you gained your knowledge of God, grace, and other spiritual doctrine from friends or from educated pastors and Bible teachers?
- Do you believe that grace has been extended to you?
- If so, have you received this gift and actually put it to use the way God intended?
- If what you know of God and the Bible confuses you, are you willing to seek a teacher or pastor to direct you?

THE TEN COMMANDMENTS WERE GIVEN SO THAT ALL COULD
SEE THE EXTENT OF THEIR FAILURE TO OBEY GOD'S LAWS. BUT
THE MORE WE SEE OUR SINFULNESS, THE MORE WE SEE GOD'S
ABOUNDING GRACE FORGIVING US.

ROMANS 5:20, TLB

Just as we invest time and energy into discovering and uncovering
truths about a potential spouse, so we must also with the one who
loved us first. Won't you consider going deep?

DAY 73

A FINE BRASSIERE
AND A GIRDLE WITH SNAP

Suck it in.

MY MOM

GROWING UP IN THE 1960s, I had a front-row seat to the final decade of the age of elegance. During the early sixties, women and girls wore gloves to church (at the very least on Easter), men wore suits (everywhere), and boys from the age of five to fifteen had every hair of their flattop haircuts greased in place with Brylcreem (I'm not sure how they ever got that stuff washed out). But nothing defined that era for me more than my mother's "foundation garments."

With her hourglass figure, Mom relied on a quality bra to hold up her girls and a girdle that removed any hint of a living, breathing person under her slip and dress. When I came of age, she introduced me to my own items of intimate apparel. The day I squeezed my chubby lower half into my girdle for the first time, she cheered me on to "suck it in," and we both fell onto the bed laughing hysterically. In those days, a woman didn't dare leave the house without being fully clothed—and that included a fine brassiere and a girdle with some snap.

There is a foundation that we as Christians can't be without as well—one that we must breathe into our minds, hearts, and souls. This foundation is defined as God's truth, spoken to us through his holy Word. When we clothe ourselves with this truth, it manifests itself in our salvation, inheritance of eternal life, and abundant life here on earth. Worn daily, this foundation provides us power against Satan, insights into righteous living, strength to conquer our negative thoughts and actions, and peace that passes all understanding. But to gain all of its benefits, we have to suck it in.

Reading God's Word but not meditating on it is like staring at a menu in the finest restaurant and never ordering the food! To receive the full benefit of his promises, we must begin by asking God to reveal himself and what he wants us to learn through our study. If we extend our minds and wills to him, he will make his teaching clear. When we study, we must seek quality of understanding rather than the quantity read. When we plow through a study, a book, or even a devotional, we often miss the lesson he longs to press on our hearts because we're rushing to complete the task rather than savor it. As we seek to understand God's Word, the Holy Spirit makes the Scripture and teaching personal, and when it's personal, then we can feel the truth coming to life. From there it's very straightforward: Pray it. Memorize it. Apply it.

- ◉ Could you improve your time in Bible study?
  - • What will benefit you most?
  - • Reprioritizing your time?
  - • Finding a quiet place to contemplate and meditate?
  - • Reading a study that challenges you?

HE WILL BE YOUR SURE FOUNDATION, PROVIDING A RICH STORE OF SALVATION, WISDOM, AND KNOWLEDGE. THE FEAR OF THE LORD WILL BE YOUR TREASURE.

ISAIAH 33:6

We are blessed beyond measure to have the privilege of speaking directly to God, extending our love, our praise, and our petition to him. Meditating on his Word simply invites him to do the same.

FUELED UP FOR THE ROAD TRIP

By failing to prepare, you are preparing to fail.
BENJAMIN FRANKLIN

I LOVE A GOOD ROAD TRIP (primarily because it allows me to take my pillow with me on vacation). I even find packing the car to be fun because I load it with treats to eat! But of course, one of the most important preparations for a road trip is filling the gas tank (this I leave to Steve). Few of us would ever strike off on the open highway with a tank half-empty, not knowing what stations are or *aren't* ahead. Those who live the abundant life know to keep their spiritual tanks filled. My friend Stacie is such a person; a mom to four children and a stepmom to one fresh out of college, she's well prepared to go the distance even in a crisis.

Stacie's first significant journey began when her firstborn, Caroline, was seven years old. Seeing Caroline lose weight and grow more lethargic each day, Stacie knew something was terribly wrong. Within hours of taking her to the pediatrician, Stacie was praying beside Caroline's hospital bed. Lewis, Stacie's husband and Caroline's dad, was out of the country on business. The other kids, ages five, three, and eleven months, were left with family. As Stacie remembers, "I did not have my husband by my side. But Jesus stepped in, and he was there for me that day in every way. . . .

"I knew that every Bible study that I had taken, every Scripture I had ever loved, and every hardship I had overcome had prepared me for this moment. We could get through this. We had our faith, and that's all we needed. Well, that and a little insulin and some modern medical devices that God so graciously provided." Because she filled her heart and mind with Scripture and the truth of God's Word long before this pilgrimage began, Stacie greeted this crisis with grace and faith and continues to all these years since, as Caroline still battles type 1 diabetes today.

Christians who live extraordinary lives react to a difficult situation with maturity and faith, knowing that Christ alone will bring them through it. They have a peace that passes all understanding—a calmness of spirit and a sense of abundance even in the middle of the chaos, confusion, and disappointment. A favorite verse Stacie turned to during this crisis is telling:

> I AM THE LORD, THE GOD OF ALL MANKIND. IS ANYTHING TOO HARD
> FOR ME?
> JEREMIAH 32:27, NIV

Stacie's go-to verse and years of study sustained her through her most trying moments and gave her an uncommon peace. Consider these questions today:

- How do you think you would cope with a life-altering diagnosis for you or someone you love?
- What is your go-to Scripture?
- What is the promise you hold on to in times of trouble?

A couple of years after Caroline's diagnosis, Stacie said to me, "I'm perfectly gifted to be the mom of a T1D child. I would feel terrible for someone else to have to struggle to research, probe, and implement treatment programs and technologies. If someone had to have this, I'm glad it's us."[14] That, my friend, is what I call a tank overflowing.

DAY 75

HAVING IT ALL

We often become mentally and spiritually barren because we're so busy.

FRANKLIN GRAHAM

MOST OF US ARE COMPLETELY winded from the constant pursuit and frantic chase of having it *all*. The notion that our personal journey will be made complete when we attain this mythical nirvana drives many a woman not to a destination of enthusiastic joy but to a place of discontentment and sometimes even depression. Having it *all* by the world's standards has long been described as having a happy marriage, well-adjusted children, a successful career, and a fulfilling personal life. This is a lot of "all" for any woman to have at any moment in time, much less spread over a lifetime. I used to say, "You can have it all, just not every day," but I was wrong. I believe we *can* have it *all* every day if we're willing to reconsider what *all* is. Spoiler alert: A tall, dark, handsome hunk of a husband who takes out the trash without being asked is not what I'm referring to.

What if we considered that having it *all* might be less about our human condition and more about our spiritual being? If we could learn to shift our mental gymnastics from the manic back handsprings of the temporal to the focused balance beam of the eternal, we might be able to see that having it all is not only achievable, but it's within our grasp.

Having it *all* is not defined by going from activity to activity to score a certain level of success, but by abiding day by day in faith and hope that God's plan is greater than our own. Having it *all* is the ability to call upon the provider of our salvation to protect how we think and act, and to show us how to pray with a spirit of thanksgiving as well as perseverance. Having it *all* is peace. Having it *all* is the opposite of being spread too thin.

Embracing the eternal version of *having it all* takes our spiritual journey to a whole new level of maturity. Moving from our "all about me" earthly toddler state, where our eyes dart from one brightly painted toy to the next, this awakening and revival gives us something solid to fix our gaze on. Oh, just like our younger selves, we'll still get distracted and chase after worldly things—we'll even bump our noggins—but unlike in our childlike state, we'll know that there is only one prize that really matters.

So how do you feel about this concept of having it all as it relates to our spiritual maturation?

- Do you chase the earthly version of having it *all* or the eternal one?
- Has your spiritual growth been stunted by distractions, or are you maturing by keeping your eyes on Christ?
- Can you see how knowing God more intimately can provide you the elements required for having it all?

LIKE NEWBORN BABIES, YOU MUST CRAVE PURE SPIRITUAL MILK SO THAT YOU WILL GROW INTO A FULL EXPERIENCE OF SALVATION. CRY OUT FOR THIS NOURISHMENT, NOW THAT YOU HAVE HAD A TASTE OF THE LORD'S KINDNESS.
1 PETER 2:2-3

When other women look at me and say, "She has it all," they're more right than they know. My *all* is eternal.

DAY 76

A NEW SET OF MARBLES

To live by grace means to acknowledge my whole life story,
the light side and the dark. In admitting my shadow side,
I learn who I am and what God's grace means.

BRENNAN MANNING, *The Ragamuffin Gospel*

I AM WHAT SOME PEOPLE call a generalist or a "jack-of-all-trades and master of none." That is, except when it comes to board games; I am an expert at Chinese checkers, the reigning family champion. I kick butt. I am so good that no one will play with me anymore; discouragement has overtaken all of my opponents (aka family members).

And just as in board games, when we're spread too thin, it can feel like every set of marbles we choose or hand of cards we've been dealt is destined to lose. We become discouraged by continuous mistakes, repeated failures, or recurring sin—all of which separate us from the abundant life.

The apostle Peter experienced what may be the most agonizing discouragement ever known. A faithful disciple of Christ, he let his guard down when he denied knowing Jesus—three times! The story (found in Matthew 26) is one of *repeated* failure. After Jesus was arrested, and while he was being interrogated by the chief priests, a servant girl approached Peter and accusingly said to him, "You were one of those with Jesus the Galilean." Can't you just see Peter rolling his eyes and waving her off as he says, "I don't know what you're talking about"? A little later on, another servant girl (where did these girls get their moxie?) said to those around her, "This man was with Jesus of Nazareth." But Peter replied, "I don't even know the man."

The third opportunity for Peter to man up came a little later when the bystanders said to Peter, "You must be one of them; we can tell by your Galilean accent."

After this third interrogation, Peter got really worked up and swore, "I don't know the man!" Then a rooster crowed.[15]

All of this, including the siren bird, had been predicted by Jesus to Peter just the night before. I can only imagine how Peter felt. I don't mind making a mistake, but when I make it over and over again, I get discouraged. But here's the good news for us and why, in a word, this story had a fabulous ending for Peter: redemption. Peter accepted forgiveness and embraced the salvation that was provided by the sacrificial blood of Christ on the cross. Peter didn't wallow in his losses or drown in disappointment. He lived a life of abundance, becoming a pillar of the early church. Christ didn't give up on Peter, and praise God that he doesn't give up on us.

As we continue to soul search for lasting peace, here are my three questions for you today:

- Is there a recurring sin or failure that you need to face? I warn you, that rooster is going to continue to crow (silently in your head) every time you do it.
- Is there a past disappointment or loss that you need to surrender in order to move on?
- Is there a failure you need to forgive yourself for in order to get back in the game?

Pick up your marbles and come back to the table; that loss doesn't define you. Sweet sister, don't get trapped in disappointment only to forfeit what is yours through Jesus. Get back in the game.

DAY 77

IT'S ALL ABOUT OUR AIM

A woman is like a tea bag—only in hot water do you realize how strong she is.
NANCY REAGAN

WHEN THE GIANT GOLIATH, who was over nine feet tall, proposed a one-on-one "throw down" to determine the victor between his "team," the Philistines, and his opponents, the Israelites, the Israelite army all but froze in fear. All, that is, except a teenage boy named David, who had happened onto the battlefield. With the utmost confidence, the lad said (and I'm paraphrasing), "No problem. I'll take him on. My God's got this."[16] Though small in stature, David was confident in God's ability to deliver him the victory because he'd seen God deliver victories to him before. David not only had a good slingshot and some smooth rocks, he knew that his aim was good—*and that God's aim was even better*!

Just as David stood before Goliath, you and I are often faced with battles of our own through a crisis or tragedy. The raging giants named Anguish, Brokenness, Despair, and Fear show up at our front door, often unannounced. If we're not prepared for their intrusion, we can find ourselves curled up in the fetal position—and even if we do see disaster heading our way, we're still often ill equipped. Oh, some of us might have a good slingshot and a few big rocks. But sister, if we want to slay these beasts, we better have spent some time improving our aim.

I have had the privilege of knowing, witnessing, and loving some of the strongest women on earth who've faced several targets: mothers who have had to release their children—either to sin or to their heavenly home; friends who have lost their husbands—either by divorce or in a fatal accident; single ladies who have lost their jobs at fifty-plus, when the job market couldn't have been worse; and one dear soul as she prepared to lose her life—when the prognosis was weeks, not months. I have marveled at these women and their ability to claim their strength through Jesus Christ. These are women who did not allow the giants from the land of pain to consume them but fought back with some of the most important attributes of the abundant life that Christ had given them: hope, confidence, and peace. These women grew stronger, not weaker, as they trusted Christ rather than their own emotions, perceptions, or rationales. They approached the Bible always searching for new rocks to hurl at the enemy and knew to call upon the power of Christ to hone their aim.

My crises have been minor compared to theirs. My prodigal son returned. I was blessed with a fabulous second husband. It's been nearly thirty years since I found myself out of work, and my one health scare was thankfully unfounded. Armed with a slingshot of truth and pebbles of faith, I've made it through these badlands of giants, but I know I can't rest on my past experience alone. I must continue to work on my aim for the day when I'm invited to face yet another giant, by investing time in reading God's Word, praying daily, giving up my battles to him, and having complete confidence in his power. I'm planning and preparing to be victorious when I come eye to eye with anguish, but I know victory doesn't come with sloppy form. I need to put into practice today all I have learned from my faith to face tomorrow's fight.

Some questions for you:

- Do you have enough rocks and a good slingshot when the giants close in on you?
- How's your aim? Are you fortifying yourself by gaining insight in God's Word, or are you relying on past practice?
- Are there giants at your door now?

He lifted me out of the pit of despair, out of the mud and the mire. He set my feet on solid ground and steadied me as I walked along.

PSALM 40:2

Our grief and despair should not rob us of the joy God has called us to experience. Oh, to be as victorious as young David was against Goliath—let's get to work on our aim.

DAY 78

ASKING THE WRONG QUESTION

A Bible that's falling apart usually belongs to someone who isn't.
CHARLES SPURGEON

EVERY SO OFTEN I have a conversation with a friend or receive an e-mail from a reader who is frustrated by a relationship, a professional challenge, or a difficult situation that she is trying to navigate. These women's words are often filled with anxiety, confusion, fear, and the persistent question "What should I do?"

I am not a licensed counselor, nor do I have formal training in theology. I have only my own personal and professional experiences, coupled with a lifetime spent between Genesis and Revelation, to draw from, but I do not need higher education to know this: The issues or challenges that are making our lives difficult will never be resolved if we rely on ourselves to solve the problem. Self-reliance is the antithesis of living the abundant life. When relationships and difficult situations are not working according to our own plans, God may be prompting us to change the question. Instead of asking, "What should I do?" perhaps a better question to consider is "What do I seek?"

I enjoy reading. I currently have my nose in five books—three business books, one historical biography, and one deeper Christian "read." Yes, I know, pretty dry stuff. But regardless of what's on my nightstand, there's one book I *study* every day. And that's the Bible. Without God's Word, I cannot, on my own, understand how to bless my family well as a wife, mother, daughter-in-law, and grandmother. Without God's counsel I cannot function well as a CEO. And as an author of Christian devotionals, I rely on his Word to keep my creative compass pointing due north, toward him. On those days when I'm confused or challenged and have to ask myself, "What should I do?" I look to Scripture to guide me, and that always directs me in prioritizing my priorities: "Seek the Kingdom of God above all else, and live righteously, and he will give you everything you need" (Matthew 6:33).

To *seek his Kingdom* means to actively read, study, and meditate on his Word to give us the wisdom and discernment required to live abundantly. *Above all else* is a clear directive to do this first: *This* is the priority, not fixing the problem at hand. When we learn more about God and his power, we can then pray and call upon that power to *live righteously*—a life that glorifies Christ. *He will give you everything you need* and more to answer that pesky question "What should I do?" His promise is this: He will do what you can't when you have your priorities straight.

Just one thought that God has placed on my heart to pose to you today:

○ Are you asking the wrong question?

DON'T WORRY ABOUT THESE THINGS, SAYING, "WHAT WILL WE EAT? WHAT WILL WE DRINK? WHAT WILL WE WEAR?" THESE THINGS DOMINATE THE THOUGHTS OF UNBELIEVERS, BUT YOUR HEAVENLY FATHER ALREADY KNOWS ALL YOUR NEEDS. SEEK THE KINGDOM OF GOD ABOVE ALL ELSE, AND LIVE RIGHTEOUSLY, AND HE WILL GIVE YOU EVERYTHING YOU NEED.

MATTHEW 6:31-33

See—I'm not making this stuff up. He already knows what you need and what you should do. As you continue this journey of soul-searching for lasting peace, seek his Kingdom first, and *what you should do* will become so apparent you can't miss it.

DAY 79

GETTING OUT OF NOWHERE

*The saved sinner . . . knows repentance is not what we do in order to earn
forgiveness; it is what we do because we have been forgiven. It serves as an
expression of gratitude rather than an effort to earn forgiveness.*
BRENNAN MANNING, *The Ragamuffin Gospel*

I HAD GONE TO VISIT a friend in East Texas whose fabulous lakeside
home is located down one long, long, looonnggg country road after
another. Thanks to her detailed directions, I had no problem getting
there. Finding my way home, however, was another story. As I came
to the end of that first looonnnggg country road, I was completely
confident that I should turn right at the next "intersection" and then
turn left at the next. But after a while, every country road began to look
the same. As I continued south, my GPS system (which was clearly just
as confused as I was) stopped talking to me altogether. As I continued
driving deeper and deeper into the middle of Nowhere, Texas, I realized I was seriously lost. It was time to stop. I had to turn around.

I believe many of us are spread too thin mentally, physically, emotionally, and spiritually because we have found ourselves in a desolate
area called Nowhere. We've reached a place where our sin takes us far
away from everyone and everything that is familiar. In Nowhere, our
minds are reeling—we begin to forget things; we can't remember which
lie we told to whom; and we allow our emotions to dictate what we
think, overriding our typical good judgment. Our mental fatigue has
turned into physical exhaustion because we haven't slept or eaten well,
and emotionally we've begun to fall apart as stress settles in for the ride
along. By the time we find ourselves deep in the middle of Nowhere,

our spiritual tanks are dry. We haven't stopped to refuel because either we feel too guilty about our sin or we want to stay in it. This leaves us with two choices: We can remain in Nowhere forever. Or we can stop and turn around.

Sister, if you're motoring into Nowhere, it's a matter of time before the road comes to a pretty dramatic end. Like my journey out in East Texas, you can either go deeper and deeper into the woods or decide it's time to acknowledge you're really lost and you need to find your way home. This is the moment on your journey when you hit the brakes and repent. That's "Bible speak" for turning around. It simply means acknowledging how lost you've become on your own, confessing your sins to God, asking for forgiveness, and committing your life to him by submitting to God's grace.

I have been hopeless and lost in Nowhere myself. But by the grace of God I found my way home. How about you?

- Is there a sin that is preventing you from leaving Nowhere?
- Do you see how this sin is consuming you mentally, physically, emotionally, and spiritually?
- What would your life look like if you stopped and turned around?

I HAVE CONSIDERED MY WAYS AND HAVE TURNED MY STEPS TO YOUR STATUTES. I WILL HASTEN AND NOT DELAY TO OBEY YOUR COMMANDS.
PSALM 119:59-60, NIV

After I stopped my car, I settled my mind, said a prayer of petition for direction, and got my bearings. I was home in no time. When you choose the abundant life, you will be too. Godspeed.

DAY 80

OWN IT—LOVINGLY

*Going to church doesn't make you a Christian
any more than going to a garage makes you an automobile.*
BILLY SUNDAY

LET'S JUST CALL A SPADE A SPADE. Or in our case, a Christian a Christian. As we continue to soul search for the abundant life, I'm pretty sure that one way to enjoy this gift that God offers us is to claim it and own it as our own, especially in the secular world.

Few enterprises welcome outspoken employees when it comes to views on religion or politics. Even in our small company, we've experienced team members over the years who were off-putting in their *zeal*. Owning our faith can be complex as we balance demonstrating God's Word without ramming it (and our personal views) down others' throats. But on the flip side, even when it's unpopular to do so, we must wear our Christian badges with pride and honor. So how do we walk this tightrope? With God's steady direction, a solid understanding of Christ's teaching, and a good filter.

As a member of the church choir during my middle school and high school years, I sang Peter Scholtes's hymn "They'll Know We Are Christians by Our Love." Every spring and summer break, we'd make a sweeping tour of our region on a hot, stinky church bus, where churches from south Texas to northern Arkansas welcomed us to lead worship services for audiences of believing and nonbelieving teenagers. As I think back on that time and how the hymn's words shaped my witness, I realize today that I was learning one of the best ways to own my faith: by respecting and loving others, regardless of their personal views. A few lines in the second stanza provide such clarity:

We will work with each other, we will work side by side
And we'll guard each man's dignity and save each man's pride
And they'll know we are Christians by our love, by our love.

It makes my heart ache for unbelievers when I see them wounded and even repulsed by Christians whose "enthusiasm" has led them to judgment, ridicule, and dismissal. Solely going to church doesn't make us good Christians; showing pride and disrespect to unbelievers doesn't either. But sharing the love of Christ just as Christ loved the sinner— well, that's not only honoring to God, that's holy.

Let me ask you . . .

- If you weren't raised in the Christian faith, how did you feel about Christians before converting?
- Were you ever made to feel unworthy, unloved, and unacceptable?
- If you are a believer, will you join me to ensure that every person, regardless of his or her past or current views, is treated with dignity and the love that Christ would extend?

Now I am giving you a new commandment: Love each other. Just as I have loved you, you should love each other. Your love for one another will prove to the world that you are my disciples.

JOHN 13:34-35

I've heard too many stories of "good Christians" whose legalistic views turned away seekers. Christ calls us to own our witness, but we don't have to be jerks about it. They will know we are Christians by our love.

DAY 81

DISTURBED

*We must allow the Word of God to confront us,
to disturb our security, to undermine our complacency
and to overthrow our patterns of thought and behavior.*

JOHN R. W. STOTT

ALTHOUGH I GREW UP attending Sunday school and worship services every week, I didn't begin to seriously study Scripture until I was about eighteen. I remember opening my Bible one cold winter afternoon and reading passages that, honestly, made me as mad as a wet hen. After about an hour of reading, I determined that Paul was not my favorite apostle. I found his teaching to be outdated for the modern day (1977). He was obviously chauvinistic, and his counsel on what I could and couldn't wear seemed completely out of left field—*no* to gold but *yes* to head coverings!? (See 1 Corinthians 11:4-5 and 1 Timothy 2:9-10.) Give me a break.

On the surface Paul may come across as if he was threatened by women and wanted to keep them in their place. But once we come to understand the customs of the time and how women were *totally* dismissed in society—especially when it came to being educated in any subject (including God's law)—we see that Paul was actually a proponent of girl power. For his time, Paul was forwarding the cause of women and raising their stature. Nonetheless, I was disturbed because I didn't have this historical and cultural background to shore up his teaching.

The Bible is sometimes a hard book to wrap our minds around. I expect, even to this day, to be rocked by something I read in the Good

Book. Because of different time periods and translations, understanding the abundant life can be complex and confusing. There will be passages that on the surface we might not understand, agree with, or know how to apply to our lives. But just because the subject matter is challenging doesn't mean we're let off the hook. We must commit to studying these passages to open our eyes to their true meaning. Rather than looking to Scripture only to comfort us in our distress or validate us when our confidence has been shaken, we must be willing to look for and open our hearts to truths that will take our relationship with Christ to the next level. We must accept the challenge to think and live differently in order to honor God and to receive the blessings that accompany righteous living.

When it comes to God's Word, where do you stand?

- Are you often disturbed, frustrated, or confused by it?
- Are you curious as to what you might not understand that will make Scripture more meaningful to you?
- Do you have a good resource to help you ferret out the historical and/or cultural details that will allow the Word of God to come alive in you?

Once I realized Paul wasn't out to make me feel bad (at least not for being a woman), I began to embrace the rich and wondrous teaching of this incredible apostle. Anyone who could write the following was clearly a precious soul:

> IF I COULD SPEAK ALL THE LANGUAGES OF EARTH AND OF ANGELS, BUT DIDN'T LOVE OTHERS, I WOULD ONLY BE A NOISY GONG OR A CLANGING CYMBAL. IF I HAD THE GIFT OF PROPHECY, AND IF I UNDERSTOOD ALL OF GOD'S SECRET PLANS AND POSSESSED ALL KNOWLEDGE, AND IF I HAD SUCH FAITH THAT I COULD MOVE MOUNTAINS, BUT DIDN'T LOVE OTHERS, I WOULD BE NOTHING. . . . THREE THINGS WILL LAST FOREVER—FAITH, HOPE, AND LOVE—AND THE GREATEST OF THESE IS LOVE.
>
> 1 CORINTHIANS 13:1-2, 13

The guy *was called* to lead us toward the abundant life that Jesus offers. When you're in the Word and think, *I don't agree with that*, that's okay. It may be a cue to look into the history and culture of the time and even think about what's happening in your own life to figure out why. After all, isn't this what soul-searching is all about?

DAY 82

DEPENDENCE DAY

God does not guide those who want to run their own life. He only guides those who admit their need of His direction and rely on His wisdom.

WINKIE PRATNEY

OVER THE PAST FEW MONTHS, I've been reading *Alexander Hamilton* by Ron Chernow. The forefathers are painstakingly introduced to the reader, along with their single-minded obsession with independence from England. And running through the veins of every red-blooded American today is the same desire for the fierce protection of our personal rights.

By nature, I have always been independent and self-governing. My predisposition for taking charge was exacerbated by having left home as a teenager. Years later as a single mom, solely responsible for the care of my children, I became further absorbed in self-sufficiency. I was completely unaware of this personality trait until I began dating Steve. Months into our marriage, Steve slowly penetrated my shell of autonomy. While he admired my independent nature and wanted me to always feel competent and capable, Steve desired for me to need him, rely on him, and rest on him. This I had to learn. In his longing to take care of me, Steve needed me to place my confidence in him and turn over to him those things that he was uniquely qualified to manage. In full disclosure, it was not hard at all for me to relinquish control of taking care of the yard, getting the oil changed, or changing the air-conditioning and furnace filters. What took years to master was remembering to ask him what he thought of my decisions *before I made them*.

If there is one area that many of us protect fiercely, it is our thoughts and opinions. I realized (and will admit that I was slow with this one) that I needed to share with Steve my ideas, desires, and goals to gain his viewpoint before acting. When we're accustomed to calling our own shots, seeking another's opinion or—hardest of all—handing over the keys so someone else can drive is not just frightening but paralyzing. To have a richly rewarding marriage, I had to place my trust in Steve. And to live a profoundly fruitful life, I must also become completely dependent on God.

God desires for us to *need* him, but he's not going to swoop in and drop the abundant life in our laps to get our attention. Instead, he promises abundant life to those who fully relinquish control. Only when we reach out to him and make a conscious decision to rely on him, surrender to him, and partner with him can we find that place where we can rest in him.

Consider these questions today:

- Are you frequently disappointed because your own resourcefulness fails you?
- Do you search for his guidance and his wisdom in every major and minor decision you make?
- Are you more dependent on him than you are on yourself?
- Which do you think will best deliver the abundant life?

I AM THE VINE; YOU ARE THE BRANCHES. IF YOU REMAIN IN ME AND I IN YOU, YOU WILL BEAR MUCH FRUIT; APART FROM ME YOU CAN DO NOTHING. . . . THIS IS TO MY FATHER'S GLORY, THAT YOU BEAR MUCH FRUIT, SHOWING YOURSELVES TO BE MY DISCIPLES.
JOHN 15:5, 8, NIV

Branches do not thrive—or even live—without being fully dependent on the vine. Christ longs for us to be his branches. What I thought I could never give over to Steve, I have, and our successful marriage is the fruit of that reliance. I've applied that same trust to my eternal partner, too, and come to find out that dependence suits me after all.

DAY 83

PLACING BLAME

*The devil abhors light and truth because
these remove the ground of his working.*

WATCHMAN NEE

WHEN WE THINK OF what drains our contentment, joy, and fruitfulness, some of us picture a person or circumstance. However, these are *not* what affect our state of abundant living. Although they're easy targets and we're great at holding them accountable, they aren't the issue. Satan is. Satan has deceived us into thinking our problems come from people, but really our problems come from him. He's quite strategic in how he goes about infiltrating and destroying relationships, and we're suckers for allowing him to manipulate us and those we care about time and again.

I can trace back every broken relationship I have to this truth. In the moment, I would have sworn that each broken relationship was due to *her* betrayal, *his* abusive tone, or *their* self-centeredness. But now I can see that the father of lies was weaving a web of disunity, cleverly disguised as a mosquito net of self-protection. If I blamed others for my hurt feelings or broken heart, I would be committed to keeping them away from me forever. Sister, Satan wants nothing more than to come after the relationships we cherish most. In her fabulous Bible study book *The Armor of God* Priscilla Shirer writes, "He [Satan] knows that you, as a daughter of God, cannot be destroyed. But he has other goals in the meantime: to distract you, discourage you, divide you from others, and disable you from experiencing everything that is rightfully yours as an adopted member of God's family."[17]

Our failure to place proper blame on Satan, who looks to multiply our insecurities and heighten our sensitivities, instead of on those we cherish and love, allows him to empty us of our relationships, both professional and personal. And oftentimes, the more God-honoring the relationship is, the more strategic the attack. The devil leaves nothing to chance if we get close to drawing others to Christ because he knows that the barren life is void of godly relationships. He'll make sure to cause division and pain wherever he can.

Might you consider placing blame where blame is due?

- Are you baffled by the sudden ending of a once healthy, sweet relationship that was dear to you?
- Have you considered that something bigger was at play than just hurt feelings?
- Knowing that Satan is at work in causing pain in your relationships, how might you stand firm against him?

STAY ALERT! WATCH OUT FOR YOUR GREAT ENEMY, THE DEVIL. HE PROWLS AROUND LIKE A ROARING LION, LOOKING FOR SOMEONE TO DEVOUR. STAND FIRM AGAINST HIM, AND BE STRONG IN YOUR FAITH. REMEMBER THAT YOUR FAMILY OF BELIEVERS ALL OVER THE WORLD IS GOING THROUGH THE SAME KIND OF SUFFERING YOU ARE.

1 PETER 5:8-9

Some people don't believe in Satan or an evil force that fights against us. Others recognize him in the grievous acts they see on the evening news, but not all of us can identify him when he's sitting between ourselves and someone we once loved. How best can we remove him and move on? Shine truth and light on him by praying for and using the power that God has provided you.

IN 160 CHARACTERS

To be yourself in a world that is constantly trying to make you something else is the greatest accomplishment.

RALPH WALDO EMERSON

IF I WERE TO ASK YOU TO write your bio in 160 characters or less, what would you write to best describe who you are? Notice I didn't say "what you do." It's easy for any of us to get lost in the temporary things we have accomplished and the minute steps we took to get there. Our job titles, our work experience, our alma maters, and our degrees often are used to define who we are. And if you're a mom, there's a likely chance that you're known as [insert name of child]'s mom. But aren't we more?

I once lost myself in my job. For a period of several years I had no earthly idea where my professional position ended and I began. I had worked in such a fast-paced, stressful environment that I identified first and foremost as vice president of merchandising. Wife and mother? Of course. Sunday school teacher? Yes, that, too. But I'll be honest—my job consumed my persona to the point that I lost track of who I truly was. Over time I realized that in order to do my job really well, I had to be someone other than my true self. I can tell you firsthand that it's physically, emotionally, and mentally depleting to try to be someone you aren't, especially when you're not totally sure who you are.

Watching the 2016 Summer Olympics, I became enthralled with US divers David Boudia and Steele Johnson. First off, anyone who can do even a front flip off the low dive is a champ in my book. But watching those two synchronize their dives at thirty-three feet in the air was amazing! I'd get dizzy and fall off the edge just standing up there on my tippy toes! But these guys magnificently pulled off two and a half somersaults with two and a half twists to win the silver medal at the Rio Games. Girlfriend, can you imagine spinning around *five* times before you hit the water? It makes me squeamish to think about.

During their postdive interviews, it became clear that these two young men were champions beyond the pool as they boldly professed their faith. Intrigued by their humility and flag-waving for Christians, I hit their Twitter feeds. How do you think these guys described themselves following this amazing display of athletic prowess? David Boudia's Twitter profile reads, "Psalm 115:1. Husband. Father. Olympic Champion Diver. Author of *Greater Than Gold*. Boilermaker." Steele Johnson describes himself as "Christ Follower. 2016 Olympic Silver Medalist. Photographer/Cinematographer. Destroyer of Haters and Lover of Prayers." I love that these two men lead with their identity in Christ as to who they are, not a shiny medal as to what they did.

I have one assignment for you today (and I'll even allow you to use more than 160 characters). On the lines below, write *who* you are:

_____

_____

_____

_____

Like me, are you curious as to what Psalm 115:1 says?

Not to us, O Lord, not to us, but to your name goes all the glory for your unfailing love and faithfulness.

One more thing these boys can add to their bios: A good witness to Ellen.

DAY 85

BECAUSE GOD SAID SO

Faith is acting like something is so, even when it's not so,
that it might be so simply because God said so.

DR. TONY EVANS

THE TOPIC OF FAITH IS a tricky one for many of us and certainly was
for me during the early months when our son was missing. For a time,
I thought if I just had enough faith, God would reward me and bring
Scott home whole and healthy. As the months turned into years, I realized that my faith was not going to alter God's will or the outcome of
our situation, but I also came to realize that my belief in an all-loving
God would provide me peace no matter the outcome. I remember
the day I decided to give up worrying that God might not "get this
right"—that he might not answer my prayer for Scott's return affir-
matively. That was the day when my Christian rubber finally met the
road. Everything I had proclaimed for my entire life and every prayer
of "Thy will be done" had to become the center of my thoughts and
actions—without exception. I had to hand my worries to him.

Thy will be done. This, my friend, clearly stated and fully accepted,
is submission. And submission is not won without faith.

I began praying "Thy will be done" as soon as I was old enough to
recite the Lord's Prayer. Throughout my young adult life, I continued
to pray this, but I know with certainty that I didn't *really* mean it. What
I meant was "Lord, I want you to want what I want and give me what
I want." Not until Scott was missing for a couple of years did I feel
God's arms of peace wrap around me in my final surrender that what
was *to be* was what God willed. My submission, born from my faith,

finally trumped my fear. But I will tell you that even now, years after Scott's return, I still get wiggly with worry. For Christians, our faith will continue to be tested throughout our lives, and it has to be renewed one crisis, one day, one prayer at a time. Learning to submit and say from our hearts "Thy will be done" will help us face our fears. In her inspiring book, *Second Chances*, Pat Smith provides readers with clarity on submission as we make plans for our lives. She writes, "I believed that in order to reach greatness, I had to do it in a certain way. I never discussed His plans for me. Now I saw why I was running but standing still . . . and why I'd never catch what I was chasing: I hadn't let Him lead the way."[18]

As you consider your state of fear versus faith today,

- Are you hoping to impress God with your faith to get the outcome you want?
- Can you exchange your anxiety for peace that God's got this?
- Is your Christian rubber meeting the road as you demonstrate your faith in the face of the unknown?

WHEN I AM AFRAID, I WILL PUT MY TRUST IN YOU.
PSALM 56:3

We must always call upon the truth we know. Our job in the face of a crisis is to be strong and patient and positive as we wait on God's direction and/or intervention, remembering that we've walked fearful paths before and he was faithful then. He will be now. Peace to you, my friend.

DAY 86

A CLOSET ROTATION

God is more concerned with conforming me to
the likeness of his Son than leaving me in my comfort zones.
God is more interested in inward qualities than outward circumstances.
Things like refining my faith and humbling my heart,
cleaning up my thought life and strengthening my character.
JONI EARECKSON TADA, *When God Weeps*

THIS YEAR WE'RE EXPERIENCING an unseasonably warm fall that has delayed my Semiannual Closet Rotation (please note that capitalization has been used because this is an *event* at my house). But I have now successfully completed boxing up my spring and summer wardrobe to make room in my closet for sweaters, jackets, and all things "cozy."

Because I am a minimalist, disorder and large assortments of *stuff* exhaust me mentally. Removing the blouses, slacks, and dresses that I won't wear when the weather turns chilly frees my mind. However, my Semiannual Closet Rotation is more than simply packing last season's apparel out of sight. Several items are discarded because they are worn clean through. Some are given away because they no longer fit well, and a few items are removed simply because they're out of style and no longer suit my taste. Every season some things have to go.

As we begin to acknowledge what can be experienced when we choose to live the life of lasting peace that Christ promises us, we find that what impedes our mental and spiritual clarity also has to go. To embrace this new season of fruitfulness and faithfulness, the things that have us spread too thin and have interfered with our walk with Christ should not be stacked in a box to be pulled out at a later date but should be completely discarded. Items such as pride, gossip, and envy should be trashed to make way for humility, restraint, and goodwill. To make room for this beautiful new wardrobe, our old, worn-out way of life must become a thing of the past. But there is a paradox to this lifestyle rotation: We cannot change without the power of Christ, but we must change to access his power. Because we cannot change without him, we must passionately run toward him, depending on him to make us new.

As you consider this rotation, what three things do you want to throw out?

Now that you've identified what's going away, what gorgeous virtues will you replace them with?

SINCE YOU HAVE HEARD ABOUT JESUS AND HAVE LEARNED THE TRUTH THAT COMES FROM HIM, THROW OFF YOUR OLD SINFUL NATURE AND YOUR FORMER WAY OF LIFE, WHICH IS CORRUPTED BY LUST AND DECEPTION. INSTEAD, LET THE SPIRIT RENEW YOUR THOUGHTS AND ATTITUDES. PUT ON YOUR NEW NATURE, CREATED TO BE LIKE GOD—TRULY RIGHTEOUS AND HOLY.
EPHESIANS 4:21-24

This year I tossed out a black turtleneck (circa 2002), a pair of faded jeans, and a dress that I can't believe I bought in the first place. I also threw out my craving for another pair of shoes, my impatience, and my complaining. I'm making room for contentment, patience, and gratitude.

ROCKING ON THE PORCH

The real friend is he or she who can share all our sorrow and double our joys.

B. C. FORBES

MY GENEROUS FRIEND Robin invited some of us from our Bible study to spend a girls' weekend at her fabulous lake house. While a few of the gals hit the Jet Skis, several of us hit the rocking chairs. Overlooking the lake, we talked as we rocked in unison with a feeling of peace that surpasses all understanding.

Some of us who gathered that weekend have been studying the Word of God together for more than ten years. We have been enlightened to new truths together; we have exposed our frailties to one another; we have prayed for and over one another during times of trials and crises; and we have rejoiced together as prayers have been answered. As we rocked on the porch that weekend, we did not leave our hectic lives, challenges, and problems behind. On the contrary, we hauled every stinkin' concern with us. When dusk settled in around us, our conversations moved from the porch to the living room. Small groups of us gathered together and shared our struggles and worries to best understand how to pray for one another. Because we have seen the physical, emotional, and spiritual evidence of God's hand in each other's lives, our faith is strengthened by one another. And that type of faith begets peace.

In years past, I have been spread too thin to attend these retreats. Business or family obligations always prevented my going. Or rather should I say, I *allowed* a myriad of things to take precedence over joining in on this time of fellowship. I see now that I robbed some of my sisters of some much-needed attention and forsook these godly women loving on me and praying over me, too!

As I came to find out, faith is often strengthened and best experienced in the company of others.

Here are a few questions for you to ponder:

- Are you spread too thin to enjoy the company of other Christian women?
- Do you see how enriched your life would be if you formed relationships with other godly women?
- Do you have a mighty prayer warrior in your life? If not, are you open to finding one?

As IRON SHARPENS IRON, SO A FRIEND SHARPENS A FRIEND.
PROVERBS 27:17

Our successes are sweeter, our joy is more abundant, and our faith grows stronger when we're part of a tribe. Don't let that frantic living keep you from rocking on the porch with your girlfriends.

DAY 88

OPTING OUT, ONCE AND FOR ALL

God creates out of nothing. Wonderful you say. Yes, to be sure,
but he does what is still more wonderful: he makes saints out of sinners.

SØREN KIERKEGAARD

I AM COVERED UP BY SPAM. Not the slimy pink meat in a can but unwanted e-mail. My business e-mail address has been sold and resold so many times that my in-box is now completely out of control. Our business has a great spam filter that works wonders, but it certainly doesn't catch them all. So every day, for about five minutes, I methodically open e-mails and click on the opt-out button. Some sites offer a selection that reads, "Never e-mail me again." I click on that one, too, for good measure. You see, when I'm done, I'm done.

There is an empowerment that comes from turning away from situations and attitudes that are unproductive, shallow, and let's just say it—sinful. Once we make up our minds to change, we can then turn our full attention toward those things that are fruitful, meaningful, and gratifying. This process takes discipline, of course, but this about-face is not something we can accomplish by sheer will. Our redemption from moral failure is realized through the saving power of Jesus Christ, and our promise of a bountiful life is realized when we mentally, emotionally, and spiritually opt out of frantic living and turn toward lasting peace.

God has blessed us with the gift of free will. He doesn't force us to accept his gift of salvation, the inheritance of an abundant life, or his lasting peace. If we like being spread too thin, then we can stay put.

But if we want a life that is flourishing, profitable, and packed with joy, we get to exercise our free will and choose him instead.

Here's your free will questions for the day:

- Do you want to live the abundant life, or is this frantic lifestyle working for you?
- Do you desire to place your trust in Jesus Christ to redeem you of your failures and empower you for righteous living?
- Are you at the end of your rope, hanging on with both hands? Can you open them wide to receive your inheritance?

THREE DIFFERENT TIMES I BEGGED THE LORD TO TAKE IT AWAY. EACH TIME HE SAID, "MY GRACE IS ALL YOU NEED. MY POWER WORKS BEST IN WEAKNESS." SO NOW I AM GLAD TO BOAST ABOUT MY WEAKNESSES, SO THAT THE POWER OF CHRIST CAN WORK THROUGH ME. THAT'S WHY I TAKE PLEASURE IN MY WEAKNESSES, AND IN THE INSULTS, HARDSHIPS, PERSECUTIONS, AND TROUBLES THAT I SUFFER FOR CHRIST. FOR WHEN I AM WEAK, THEN I AM STRONG.

2 CORINTHIANS 12:8-10

We can't opt out alone; we're just too weak. But his grace is more than sufficient to help us let go of that rope—once and for all.

DAY 89

THE PRACTICE OF
ABUNDANT LIVING

It is a mistake to think that the practice of my art has become easy to me.
I assure you, dear friend, no one has given so much care to the study of
composition as I. There is scarcely a famous master in music whose
works I have not frequently and diligently studied.

WOLFGANG AMADEUS MOZART

STEVE AND I HAVE FRIENDS who practice medicine. We also have friends who practice law. Although neither profession is known for its humility, I love our friends' transparency! They claim right out loud that they haven't yet mastered their fields of expertise. They make mistakes, learn from those mistakes, apply that learning, and move on.

Although I know about the abundant life and can write about it and speak intelligently to it, I humbly admit I haven't mastered it yet either. You may be there too. Like Mozart and my doctor and lawyer friends, we must return to our study every day. Solely reading this devotional on embracing the abundant life will not completely transform us, just as reading a book on Mozart will not make us famous composers. We're going to have to pray hard, focus, be diligent, and get ourselves back on the horse when we fall off. Because we will.

We must persevere through the process. We have succeeded in life, and we have failed; we have wounded others, and we've been hurt. We have been frustrated and angry and confused as we've struggled against our brokenness. We have even felt abandoned by God. When I first read the words of Christ on the cross, "My God, my God, why have you forsaken me?"[19] I was too young to understand the depths of this despairing cry. Not until I was face down on my living room floor praying for the return of my son did I fully grasp these words and realize that Christ knew exactly what I was feeling. He had lived it and was there to comfort me, if I would only let him. We are never closer to God than when we are dangling at the end of our rope; when we have no more fixes, options, or recourse. When our hands are bloody and our grips are weak, that's when he does his greatest work in our lives. But we have to be willing to let go—and begin again the practice of abundant living.

Practice will not perfect us because we're all flawed sinners, saved by grace. But putting into action the elements and virtues of abundant living will make us happier, will make us better, and will make us living examples of the love of Christ. The questions you must consider are . . .

- When circumstances spread you thin, will you pray for God to fortify your spirit?
- If you have become discouraged by your failure, will you decide today to persevere?

DEAR BROTHERS AND SISTERS, ONE FINAL THING. FIX YOUR THOUGHTS ON WHAT IS TRUE, AND HONORABLE, AND RIGHT, AND PURE, AND LOVELY, AND ADMIRABLE. THINK ABOUT THINGS THAT ARE EXCELLENT AND WORTHY OF PRAISE. KEEP PUTTING INTO PRACTICE ALL YOU LEARNED AND RECEIVED FROM ME— EVERYTHING YOU HEARD FROM ME AND SAW ME DOING. THEN THE GOD OF PEACE WILL BE WITH YOU.

PHILIPPIANS 4:8-9

No one is perfect and all will fail. Some will give up, but many will soldier on. I hope you join me on the field.

DAY 90

READY TO LET GO?

OVER THE PAST NINETY DAYS, you've done a lot of work. *Important work.* Reconditioning your heart, retraining your mind, and strengthening your body is a significant undertaking but entirely worth it to cash in on the abundant life. So we come to the payout—the place where we bare our souls to our almighty God and commit to living a more rewarding, fulfilling life for however many days we walk this earth. Here you are. And here he is.

- Have you laid claim to your rightful inheritance of an abundant life?
- Will you commit to righteous living as the path to an excellent life well lived?
- Will you invest time in learning the Word of God to know him better?
- Will you identify yourself, first and foremost, as a Christ follower?
- Will you pray for others and allow them to pray for you in order to build a faith that results in lasting peace?
- Will you let go of that rope you've been holding on to for dear life and allow yourself to fall into his arms?

O GLORIOUS GOD,

We come before you, enthralled by your power and grace. That you would extend to us such a beautiful and fulfilling life on earth is evidence of your faithful love!

We are embarrassed that we have failed to let in your light, study your Word, and follow your guidance. We've forfeited our faith in you by worrying incessantly, when all the while your perfect plan and will for our lives has been playing out. Forgive us, O Lord, for our spiritual and moral failures.

Thank you for your Word, your guidance, your grace, and your power to live life abundantly. Your promise of lasting peace as you grow us spiritually by showing us how to know you and love you better is a gift beyond words. Thank you for caring enough about us to disturb and convict us through your teaching.

We give ourselves over to you and ask that you transform us to your design as we rotate our old selves out to make way for the new. Strengthen us in our walk and our witness to those around us. Give us courage when you call on us to act and discernment to know when to pull back. Refresh us in our service and ministries to others.

Provide us, Father, with the tools we need to claim the inheritance you've promised of an abundant life. Fortify us to opt out of this frantic living, once and for all. In the name of the Father, the Son, and the Holy Spirit, we pray expectantly for your lasting peace. Amen.

ABOUT THE AUTHOR

ELLEN MILLER is the author of *The One Year Book of Inspiration for Girlfriends . . . Juggling Not-So-Perfect, Often-Crazy, but Gloriously Real Lives* and *Lord, Have Mercy: Help and Hope for Moms on Their Last Nerve.* Prior to writing, she enjoyed a thirty-year career serving as an officer for a Fortune 500 company and as the founder and CEO of a successful marketing company. Throughout her marketing career, Ellen was a key contributor to the launch of some of the most important technologies and products of our time for Global 100 technology brands. Today, she embraces the opportunity to inspire women from all walks to dream audaciously, work purposefully, and live abundantly.

Living in Dallas, Ellen enjoys life to the fullest with her husband, Steve, as well as their two grown children, son-in-law, and granddaughter.

May the love of God fill your heart as you love others.
May the will of God fill your mind as you discern your way.
And may the peace of God cover you and yours . . . from head to toe!

NOTES

1. John 10:10, ESV, emphasis added
2. Stephen A. Diamond, "Anger Disorder (Part Two): Can Bitterness Become a Mental Disorder?" *Evil Deeds* (blog), *Psychology Today*, June 3, 2009, https://www.psychologytoday.com/blog/evil-deeds/200906/anger-disorder-part-two-can-bitterness-become-mental-disorder.
3. Scripture passages are taken from the NIV.
4. Jerry Bridges, *Respectable Sins: Confronting the Sins We Tolerate* (Colorado Springs, CO: NavPress, 2007), 151.
5. Ibid., 149.
6. National Geographic website, s.v. "air pollution," http://nationalgeographic.org/encyclopedia/air-pollution/.
7. Joe Tacopino, "'Bowled' Over! NY Family Buys Bowl for $3—It Sells for $2 Million," *New York Post*, March 20, 2013, http://nypost.com/2013/03/20/bowled-over-ny-family-buys-bowl-for-3-it-sells-for-2-million/.
8. James 4:1, NIV
9. I'm referring to the fruit of the Spirit, mentioned in Galatians 5:22-23.
10. See Matthew 7:3-5.
11. Romans 8:5-6, NIV
12. "The State of American Vacation: How Vacation Became a Casualty of Our Work Culture," Project: Time Off, http://www.projecttimeoff.com/research/state-american-vacation-2016.
13. Brother Lawrence, *The Practice of the Presence of God* (New Kensington, PA: Whitaker House, 1982), 55.
14. Although I'm very close with Stacie and Caroline's story, I want to extend a very special thank-you to our friend Julie Thomas for interviewing Stacie and getting her word-for-word perspective. You can read more about Stacie and Caroline's journey at http://littlefarmstead.blogspot.com/2015/05/faith-for-farm-diabetes-type-1.html.

15. The quoted verses are from Matthew 26:69-75.

16. This quotation is modified from 1 Samuel 17:32-37. The entire story of David and Goliath is found in 1 Samuel 17.

17. Priscilla Shirer, *The Armor of God* (Nashville, TN: Lifeway Press, 2015), 23.

18. Pat Smith, *Second Chances: Finding Healing for Your Pain, Regaining Your Strength, Celebrating Your New Life* (Bloomington, MN: Bethany House Publishers, 2016), 78.

19. Matthew 27:46, esv

JUST WHEN YOU THINK YOU'VE GOT THIS MOTHERHOOD THING DOWN . . .

- Your toddler expresses his inner Picasso on your freshly painted walls . . . in permanent marker.
- Your fourteen-year-old demonstrates her newly acquired modeling skills . . . via every social network known to man.
- Your husband pulls up in a new car that you can't afford . . . and that has only two seats.

Lord, have mercy. What are they thinking?

ELLEN MILLER

Lord, Have Mercy

Help and hope for moms on their last nerve

While motherhood is often a hysterical ride of pure joy, it can also hold some of the most mind-numbing, heartbreaking, and sacrificial moments of your life. In *Lord, Have Mercy*, popular author Ellen Miller writes to moms as they live through the trials and triumphs of parenting in the twenty-first century. All too real, always honest, and often hilarious, this devotional is filled with personal stories to remind you that God is with you in both the big and the small moments of motherhood.

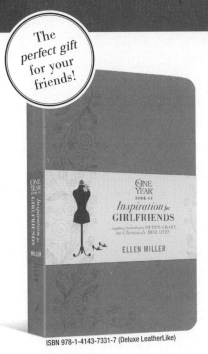
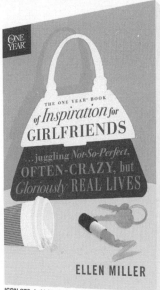